Echoes From Down Under

by

Herb Williams

Dedication

This book is dedicated to Sharon, my wife, intrepid companion, and priceless critic; and to my Australian friends and contributors, especially Denis and Beth McDermott, Kathie and Ray Hyland, and PattyAnn Ellis.

Other books by Herb Williams

Easy Writing Across the Curriculum
or Anywhere Else

North to Alaska with a No-Account Cat

Only the Faces Change (A High School Odyssey)

Where the Crown, Kilt & Shamrock Take You

Table of Contents

Acknowledgements

Many thanks to the following: Thomas Harrigan, travel professional at Laura's Travel Service in Redlands, who arranged for a perfect trip; Tauck Tours for an exciting and informative journey; tour director Ron Wesner, whose guidance was enlightening and humorous; bus driver, Roger, whose friendliness and expertise made our tourism cordial and safe; thirty-eight "mates," who added sociability to the trip, especially Fred and Louise Moritz whose friendship still endures; my editor, Becky Arrants, whose expertise made this book a better read; and cover designer, Kathy Snapp, whose talent and creativity are exceptional.

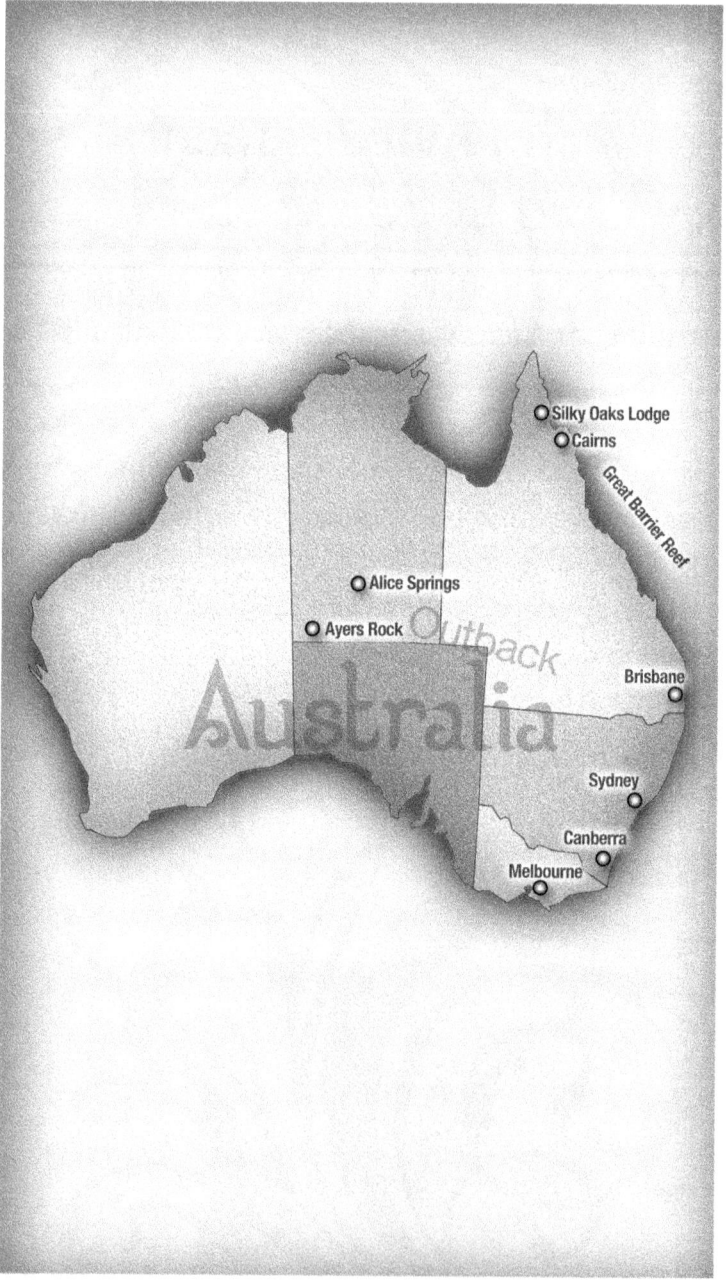

Silky Oaks Lodge
Cairns

Great Barrier Reef

Alice Springs
Ayers Rock

Outback

Australia

Brisbane

Sydney

Canberra

Melbourne

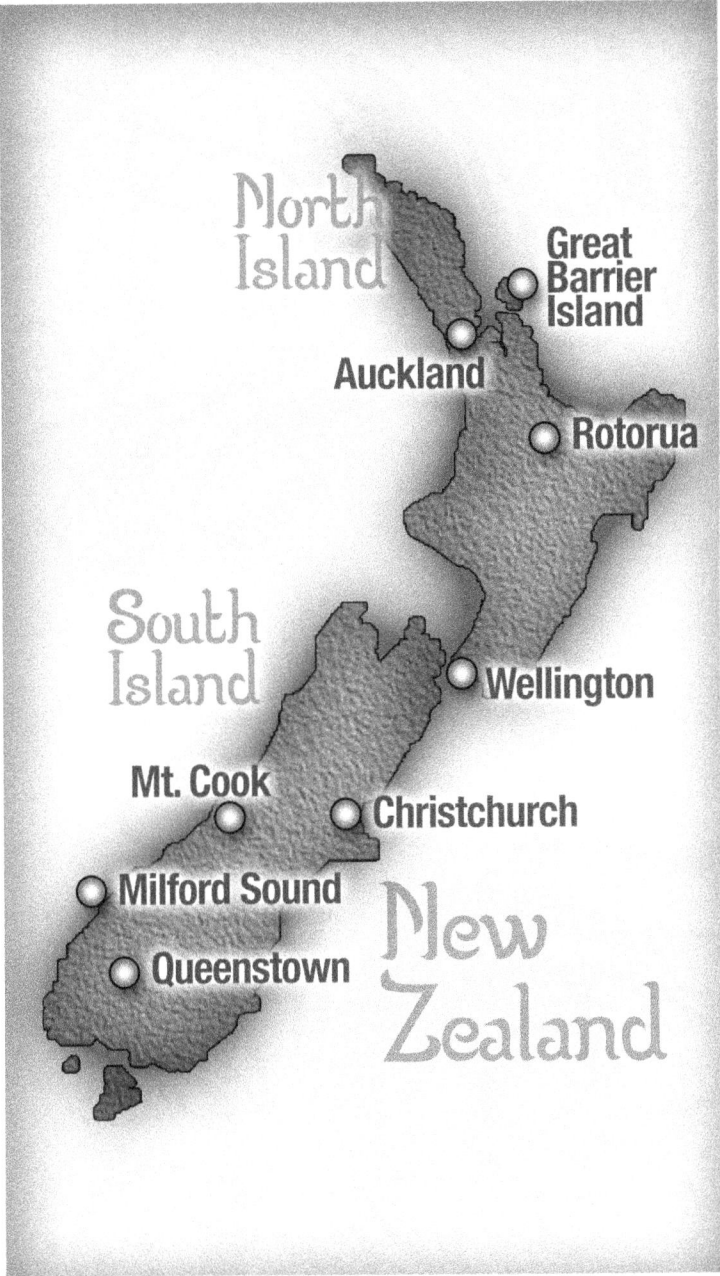

North
Island

Great
Barrier
Island

Auckland

Rotorua

South
Island

Wellington

Mt. Cook

Christchurch

Milford Sound

New
Zealand

Queenstown

Introduction

My wife, Sharon, and I linked up with Tauck Tours for a sixteen-day air and land excursion throughout much of Australia and most of New Zealand. We flew from Los Angeles, California, to Melbourne, Australia. It was a long flight in more ways than one. It took almost fourteen hours during which we lost a day and the ability to sleep.

After arriving in Melbourne, we met Ron Wesner, our tour director and were transported to the Langham Hotel. Soon after we checked in, we left for a river cruise on the Yarra River.

On our return, we dressed for dinner—the latest tourist chic—and left to board the burgundy colored, Colonial Tramcar Restaurant, an 1891 bistro on wheels.

The next morning, we took a bus tour throughout the city. In the residential areas, two-story houses sporting wrought iron, balcony grillwork, intermingled with narrow, long, one-story houses. Several times, the bus was involved with the infamous Melbourne Hook—the wackiest right turns anywhere.

As we travelled along, Ron entertained us with stories of some of the famous Melbourne personalities, including Nellie Melba and Ned Kelly.

At the Shrine of Remembrance, a memorial to all Australians who served in war, we gathered at the World War II forecourt near a tall granite pillar inscribed with the names of the defense forces, and the theatres of war in which they served. As I wandered about observing fateful memorabilia, the strains of "And the Band Played Waltzing Matilda" drifted throughout the vaulted hall.

We departed our bus tour at the Altman Cherney opal establishment in the downtown district, the center of the opal trade. A salesman, eager to show us around, opened a huge safe that displayed the largest opal in the world.

We stopped for coffee inside the nineteenth century Queen Victoria Market, the largest open-air market in the Southern Hemisphere. It was our first experience with ordering coffee in Australia. I read the menu above and behind the counter of a small coffee bar. Listed, were the usual espresso delights. Also listed were the designations, "short black, long black, flat white," and "Americano."

I paid the check with an Australian twenty-dollar bill, and received exact change since no pennies exist in Australia. Everything comes out even or is rounded off to the next five cents.

After our stay in Melbourne, we flew to Alice Springs, and were bussed to a dreamtime station near an Aboriginal camp to meet with Mark Stewart, who gave us insights into the Aboriginal culture and their stories of creation put into songs—the only way their language remains constant. They have no written language, simply an oral language that changes over time.

When the lecture was over, Ron, getting into the spirit, ate a witchetty grub (a large, white, wood-eating larvae of the cossid moth), and two other guys did the same. They all said the larva tasted like fresh corn. When they offered one of the wiggling insects to me, I respectfully declined.

After the disgusting grub-crunching demonstration, we enjoyed a *corroboree*, an Australian Aboriginal dance ceremony.

At a prescribed time, we entered a theater to watch a multimedia presentation of the Dreamtime: a concept of "time out of time," or "everywhen," inhabited by ancestral figures, often of heroic proportions or with supernatural abilities.

Before dawn the next morning we rode into total darkness (there are no street lights in the Australian outback) to find two hot air balloons in which we were to sail through the sky.

Later that day, we flew to Ayers Rock, and drove to Uluru–Kata Tjuta National Park. In the distance, Uluru (Ayers Rock) rose abruptly from the scrubland. One of Australia's most recognizable natural landmarks, Uluru looms 1,150 feet above the flat desert landscape, and is about 2.2 miles long, 1.2 miles wide and over five miles in circumference. Australian Aboriginal stories are recorded in the fissures, cliffs, and caves of the rock itself.

At the beginning of our tour of Uluru, I was reluctant to cover my face with a fly net attached to a wide brimmed hat (not the most fashionable accessory), but quickly realized my mistake. Hundreds of the most persistent flies in the world tried to suck moisture off of me, especially from the backs of my hands, my face, ears, nose, and even my tongue if I didn't keep my mouth shut.

That same day, we flew to Cairns, boarded our coach, and traveled up the Captain Cook Highway. The very scenic road winds alongside the coast between the reef and rainforest of tropical Queensland, forty-seven miles from Cairns to Mossman. According to the pundits, its ocean views and mountain background make it one of the best drives in the country.

We arrived at Silky Oaks Lodge, and were given our room assignments, keys, and a guide to lead us to individual tree houses. In the crocodile cluster (cabanas not predators), we climbed a few steps to enter our bungalow. I opened the door to a beautiful, bright interior, walked across a shiny multi-colored hardwood floor, and was blown away by a large, inviting bed, a marble bathroom with a walk-in rain shower and large corner double spa-bath.

After our repast, it was off to Port Douglas to board the *Quicksilver*, a huge catamaran bound for the Great Barrier Reef, the world's largest coral reef system composed of over 2,900 individual reefs and 900 islands stretching over 1,400 miles covering an area of approximately 133,000 square miles.

I was looking forward to arriving at a sun-soaked golden beach, riding on a glass bottom boat, and enjoying an open bar under waving palm trees. Instead, we moored at an immense floating ship-like platform—a metal monstrosity. Several water activities were available, but since Australia seems to have a corner on the most deadly varieties of sea life, I was glad I didn't have a bathing suit. I had no desire to be stung or stabbed to death, or eaten alive.

Later, we arrived at Hartley's Creek Crocodile Farm for an exciting visit with Goldie, Bob, and a bunch of other crocs that shall remain nameless.

After leaving the crocodile farm, with our new knowledge of croc feeding and sexual habits, we visited Tjapukai Aboriginal Park where we observed authentic Stone Age artifacts, witnessed a live rendition of an ancient celebration of song and dance, and watched a film that illustrated the painful story of what happened when the modern world descended upon a 40,000 year-old culture.

Later, we walked out to an open area to experience the thrill of throwing a boomerang. Most of the men got the hang of it, but the ladies had trouble sailing the boomerang outward and in most cases threw it into the ground. It was a laughable experience.

We left Cairns onboard an early morning Qantas Airlines flight into cloudy and drizzly Sydney. Upon arrival, we boarded a comfortable OPAL coach for a drive around the city.

Our first stop, Bondi Beach, was advertised as:

AUSTRALIA'S MOST FAMOUS BEACH, A CURVING GOLDEN STRETCH OF PALE GOLD SAND AND TURQUOISE WAVES, ATTRACTING BEACH BUNNIES, SURFER DUDES AND BEACH LOVERS ALIKE.

I wasn't impressed. Maybe because it was a wet, grey day and the beach, promenade, and shops were empty of day-trippers.

Later, we strolled along a well-worn path, from Kings Cross to Mrs. Macquarie's Chair, high above Sydney Harbour (in deference to the Australian spelling), catching glimpses along the way of the Harbour Bridge, Opera House, and Garden Island Navy Base where the Royal Navy has docked since the early nineteenth century.

Back on the bus, it was a short ride to the Gap, a dip in the sandstone cliffs at the South Head peninsula facing the Tasmanian Sea.

There, we walked down a footpath, but not the one I would have chosen—the 1870s cobblestone trail that leads to Lady Bay Beach, one of three in Sydney where nude bathing is lawful.

Although the cliff is a popular visitor destination, given the easy access, and its dramatic location at the extreme edge of the city, it has gained infamy for suicides.

Later that afternoon, we journeyed from the heights to the depths—the Central Business District (CBD)—popularly referred to as "town" or "the city," a suburb and main commercial center of Sydney, one of the oldest established areas in the country.

Since Sharon and I were not in a shopping mood, we moved on to the busy heart of the city—Hyde Park, where we were welcomed by great mounds or bowls of luxurious, blooming flowers, and thousands of trees.

Monuments dotted the landscape, including the beautiful ANZAC Memorial dedicated to remembering all Australians who have served their country.

Then, it was on to life on "The Rocks," a jumble of cobblestone streets and cul-de-sacs just five minutes from Circular Quay, pronounced "key." (How the Australians get that pronunciation, I will never know).

The area was settled by convicts who, like others, colonized Australia when Britain (after the US Declaration of Independence), could no longer send misfits and criminals to the American colonies.

That afternoon, we boarded a boat for a cruise of Sydney Harbour, which was somewhat boring. It looked like every other harbor in the world except for the Opera House, the Harbour Bridge, and Fort Denison Island.

We disembarked at Circular Quay, a popular neighborhood for both locals and tourists, consisting of walkways, pedestrian malls, parks, and restaurants. It also serves as a transport exchange for rail, bus, and ferries.

The next day, the group took advantage of a guided tour of the Opera House, shaped like the filled sails of a schooner, or less romantically—like egg shell quarter sections—that curve over large, cathedral-like windows tinted to deflect sunlight. At a distance, the "sails" manifest a solid white exterior, but up close, thousands of small, ceramic tile squares defeat that look.

When I left the Opera complex, I looked upward at the Sydney Harbour Bridge, its steel plates and girders anchored by massive stone blocks looked every bit like its nickname—the "Coat Hanger." My gaze tracked the expanse of one of the longest and tallest arch-spanning bridges in the world. Even large boats plied the harbor with plenty of room to spare.

Later, we drove across the Coat Hanger to visit the Taronga Zoo. Four volunteer docents met us and divided us into small groups. Our guide chose the Australian section to visit first, and as it turned out, last for me. The zoo was just too damned big.

Australia monopolizes the strange animal world, especially the egg laying mammals such as the platypus that, like some pubescent youngster doesn't know what he wants to be.

The next day David and PattyAnn Ellis picked us up and drove us to Olympic Park where several huge towers, thirty to forty feet high, like copies of the robot, Iron Mike, lined the main boulevard, offering testament to former Olympic sites, including Los Angeles, Munich, and Melbourne.

Later we visited Featherdale Wildlife Park that houses the world's largest collection of native Australian animals, and cares for over 2,200 animals, birds, and reptiles, including a twenty-foot crocodile. Well…he looked that long.

The following morning, we boarded the coach and headed for the Sydney airport to leave Australia for New Zealand.

But first an aside: Years ago, I had previously visited Canberra, the capital of Australia, and Brisbane, one of that nation's oldest cities.

Canberra was selected for the location of the nation's capital in 1908 as a compromise between rivals Sydney and Melbourne. It is unusual among Australian cities, being an entirely planned city outside of any state, similar to Washington, D.C.

After filling my eyes with the panoramic present, I descended into the historic past—the Australian War Memorial that commemorates the brave soldiers who fought and died in various conflicts and also provides a living and interesting history of the nation's engagement in wars, from the colonial period to the present day.

We took advantage of a free, guided tour of the two houses of parliament, similar to the British House of Commons. At the Parliament House, we were supposed to see democracy in action, but Parliament was not in session. Unlike the US Congress, where members show up when they feel like it, in capital Canberra, Parliament meetings are compulsory.

The hotel in Brisbane was a short walk to the heart of the municipality where South Bank's cultural institutions and restaurants met riverside gardens.

The next morning, we visited the American Amphibious Base. From there, it was a short trip to the Lone Pine Koala Sanctuary where we donated money to pay for holding a koala.

Back to the future: We bid farewell to Australia, flew across the Tasmanian Sea and landed in Auckland, situated north of almost everything on the North Island of New Zealand.

After lunch, we toured Auckland, first down Queen Street and then along the waterfront. Stretched out for what seemed like miles, Queen Street hosts a wide variety of stores, shops, banks, and restaurants.

It wasn't far to the Auckland War Memorial Museum that dominates the skyline while sitting prominently on the crater rim of a dormant volcano in the Auckland Domain, a large public park.

Nearby, the Māori cultural show, included in our tour, delivered prodigious grunting, stomping, and threatening, with exceptionally long tongue wagging from the male dancers, as opposed to the females who gracefully danced, moved their hands and arms, and twirled their balls to and fro.

The next day we visited archeologist and diver, Kelly Tarlton's Sea Life Aquarium, set on the waterfront of Okahu Bay. There, he built a 360-foot tunnel created from disused sewage storage tanks. He also developed a new method of building an acrylic lining, which allowed 360-degree viewing rather than flat panel observations.

We stepped onto a people-mover that slowly proceeded in a wide circle. I looked up as fish sashayed over my head. It was a weird feeling—almost as if I was scuba diving, yet unencumbered with tanks, mask, and rebreather.

Before we returned to the hotel, we departed the bus at the base of the Sky Tower, a 1,076-foot tall observation and telecommunications edifice, reminiscent of Seattle's Space Needle. We avoided the casino, restaurants, and live theater at the lower levels, and rode an elevator up to the main observation level at 610 feet just below the restaurant, which turns 360 degrees every hour.

From Auckland, we traveled by coach through lush farmlands into the scenic heart of the North Island. We stopped for lunch at Longlands Farm, a combination working farm and country garden, where I learned more than I wanted to know about dairying, calving, breeding, and even sweetbreads.

After lunch, we visited the world famous Agrodome near Ngongothaha (a place where you can go to a have a good laugh) to learn everything about sheep farming. Well, almost everything.

As we drove up, sheep, as if to greet us, gathered at the fences that lined the roadway, but the cows couldn't have cared less. They were a mixed bag (no pun intended), such as Herefords, Jerseys, Guernseys, and "Oreos"—black on both ends with a wide white striped middle.

We disembarked from the bus, entered the Agrodome, a huge farm shed, and found a place to sit on one of the long wooden benches. Nineteen breeds of sheep, all rams, entered the stage, one by one, and found their place behind placards that described their breed. No confusion ensued, since the rams had accomplished this feat so many times before.

Some pundit once said "New Zealand is a country of eighty million sheep, four million of which think they are human."

Then, it was off to Rotorua. With some trepidation, we left the bus to walk through a small version of Yellowstone called the Whakarewarewa Thermal Village, now called Te Puia, which is much easier to pronounce.

Prone to geothermal activity from deep within the Earth's core, sulfur dioxide seeps through cracks and craters and fills the air with an acrid stench. Amid the smoking rifts and seething pools, boiling mud bubbles, and steaming geysers shoot high into the sky. Water oozes down otherworldly, scorched white terraces. Pools and lakes take on hues of blue, green, pink, and yellow.

We left the land of geysers, no telling when they would go off—much like our warrior guide to the Māori Cultural Center. Tattooed from head to toe, wearing the smallest of loincloths, he was threatening, thrusting and waving a spear, stomping from side to side, and sticking out his large tongue, but then he smiled and I knew we were not to be sacrificed to some ancient god, so we followed him. I'm sure the women in the group enjoyed the rear view.

Landing at the non-descript airport near Mount Cook, we exited the plane, collected our luggage, and entered a small building just large enough to provide a waiting area and restrooms.

At 12,218 feet, Mount Cook/Aoraki is the highest mountain in New Zealand. It lies in the Southern Alps, the mountain range which runs the length of the South Island.

We stayed at the Hermitage Hotel at the base of Mount Cook. Far from being a hermitage, the five star, ten story hotel is built like a chalet, with satellite cabins for backpackers and others who want to "rough it."

On a subsequent flight, we disembarked the plane, boarded a waiting bus, and departed for the Te Anau Hotel and Villas.

The following morning we were off to Te Anau the main jumping off place for the glacier-carved wilderness that is Fiordland National Park, and Milford Sound, the main attraction in the park.

The scenic 2.5-hour drive to the sound was incredible. The weather was mostly overcast, but at times sunlight shined through to illuminate granite ramparts that ascended high into the cloudy sky—a massive backdrop of dark, foreboding gray to countless waterfalls that rushed down the sheer rock faces.

The next day, we traded our bus ride for a lengthy, pleasant, but not spectacular, boat ride across Lake Te Anau to the Te Anau Caves where we descended underground to join a guided adventure by path and small punt through limestone caverns to a glowworm grotto.

Then, it was on to Kingston, a small town on the southern shores of crystal clear Lake Wakatipu. There, we paused just long enough to look over the vintage steam train called the *Kingston Flyer*—but not to ride it.

We moved on to Arrowtown, New Zealand's only living historic gold mining settlement built on the banks of the Arrow River, once a rich source of gold.

After lunch, we found our way to the Karawau River Bridge where fearless bungee jumpers dove head first from the overpass to just inches above the water, some one hundred forty-two feet below.

Then, we moved on to the Sky Ride, a gondola journey, reputed to be the steepest lift in the Southern Hemisphere. The five minute ride to the top of Bob's Peak was exhilarating as the view expanded to a remarkable two hundred twenty degree panoramic vision of Lake Wakatipu and Queenstown, accentuated by several towering peaks.

At the bottom terminal of the Skyline ride, Sharon and I "birthed" from the egg-like carriage. Looking left, I saw our group near a metal tunnel, the entrance to the Kiwi Birdlife Park.

Ron waived us over and the assemblage entered the sanctuary to slow down for a bit and take in the beauty of the natural world.

It was a short walk down a flight of steps into beautiful gardens including native trees, and ponds that enticed waterfowl. Under dappled shade, we strolled throughout the park to observe many of New Zealand's famous birds as well as the tuatara.

Another flight and landing left us adrift to tour Christchurch, the most English city outside of the UK.

Outside of our hotel, an ancient tram, from out of the turn of the twentieth century, lumbered up. When it stopped, we grabbed the handrail, climbed the high steps, and stood next to the driver. He said, "You can ride all day and get off and on when you want."

We hopped off at the art center; a maze of studios, art galleries, theaters, cinemas, cafes, restaurants, and small shops selling everything from oil paintings to handmade crafts.

The next day, we punted in a narrow, flat bottom boat on the Avon which is Gaelic for river. Often tourists and others add "River" to Avon, which creates the repetitious tag: "River River."

As the punt arrived, the punter, dressed in traditional Edwardian attire, helped Sharon into the boat, but I was on my own. I stepped into the vessel expecting it to rock, threatening a dip in the water, but the flat bottom kept it steady while I moved into position. It was a long way down, and I had some anxiety with my ability to rest my butt on the seat.

Later, after another tram ride, we found ourselves in Cathedral Square. Locally known simply as the Square, the geographical center and heart of Christchurch, which has long been a community focal point; a place where people come together in good times and bad, and a backdrop for scores of significant historical events. The wide-open plaza fronted and surrounded the turn of the nineteenth century Anglican Cathedral.

The next day, we rode the tram to Christchurch Botanic Gardens that sprawled over an area of fifty-two acres adjacent to the "River River" loop.

The Gardens display a variety of exotic and local plants of New Zealand, and collections of florae from all around the world including Asia, North America, Europe, South America, and South Africa.

The highlight of this beautiful place is the begonia garden. Except for Monet's Garden near Paris, I have never seen so much beautiful color in one place—a vast array of vibrant colors, marked by placards that identified the varieties.

In the evening, we gathered for the last time as a group for a farewell dinner at the Canterbury Tales restaurant. The cuisine was International, New Zealand, and Japanese—take your pick—and the dress was smart casual. My clothing was casual but far from smart—too many times packed and unpacked.

Chapter 1

Memorable Melbourne

I hate flying about as much as I hate eating liver. Actually, the flying isn't as onerous as departing from LAX (Los Angeles International Airport).

In preparation for our flight to Australia, the labyrinth, as usual, was crowded and confusing even though we were flying out on the "red-eye." Foolish me, I thought that since we were leaving close to midnight that the airport would be less mobbed. No such luck.

For matters of security, known only to airport personnel, we had to stand in two lines, the first to receive our boarding passes and have our luggage weighed and tagged, and the second to have both suitcases scanned.

After I received the boarding passes, and before I left the counter, I reviewed the seat assignments and noticed that they were not contiguous.

I said to the clerk, "These seats are not next to each other."

She said, "Yes, they are. They are aisle seats directly across from each other."

I couldn't figure out the non sequitur of how we could be sitting together while separated, so I said, "Please exchange these seats for two that are right next to each other."

She said, "Okay," and completed the exchange.

We then reloaded our suitcases back onto a cart and wheeled them to the next challenge, a long line that traveled from the only scanner available through several switch backs to the terminal entrance and beyond.

I calculated that if we moved in this line at what looked like a snail's pace, we would miss our flight. However, we were saved from that fate because of the cane Sharon was using for support during the last stages of her recuperation from a knee replacement. A line attendant noticed the cane, and told us to step up to the front of the line, a privilege offered to the handicapped.

Our luggage passed inspection and was sent to the proper loading designation with plenty of time to spare, and we were on our way to the subsequent hurdle—scans of our bodies and hand-carried stuff. Of course, Sharon's titanium knee set off alarms, subjecting her to a more rigorous inspection.

When we found our seats on the plane, I suddenly realized my gaffe: a failure, at times, to listen to my wife. During the fuss about the seat arrangements, Sharon kept insisting that the aisle seats were okay.

Unfortunately, our swapped seats, the only ones available, were directly across the aisle from the airplane's nursery section, complete with changing facilities and miniature fold out bunks.

The intent of these amenities was to provide parents, and everyone else on board, relief from the stress of travelling with babies or tots. However, on this flight the opposite was true. Two toddlers, whom I named Cry and

Yelp, ruined the whole plan. They screamed and cried throughout the fifteen-hour flight whenever they were accommodated with a change of diapers—or an attempt to bed them down. When one of them wasn't fraying nerves, the other one took up the cause.

It was after midnight and both of the little "darlings" should have been asleep. Lord knows no one else was sleeping. I tried to block out the piercing screams with headphones and a continuous watch of a small TV screen secured to the back of the seat in front of me. It didn't work.

After I watched all that was available on TV, I concentrated on the fact that we had crossed the International Date Line, and that a whole day was lost. It was too bad that Cry and Yelp hadn't also been lost. Out of desperation, I opened the window shade to stare into the darkness. As time passed, my gawk was enhanced when the sun rose out of the blackness, briefly rode the horizon, and then disappeared again.

By the time we landed, I had exhausted all of my diversions, including recollecting a trip I had taken to Australia some eleven years ago:

> As the plane approached Sydney, I looked out the window and saw a huge dark mass hanging over the city. At the same time, I heard the voice of the captain, "Because of the threat of a violent storm, we will have to divert to Melbourne."
>
> I took another look to confirm the menace. Ironically, the sky was clear up and down the coast, but

for some reason, known only to God and weathermen, the huge, black clouds pinpointed Sydney.

When we landed in Melbourne, passengers were instructed to remain seated while attendants disinfected the airplane. We sat while they walked down the aisle, with aerosol cans in hand, one attendant spraying overhead and another spraying underneath the seats. Once the disinfectant mist cleared, we were allowed to exit the plane.

After a four-hour layover, we boarded the same plane for our flight back to Sydney. When we arrived, we endured the same disinfectant ritual. I was sure that if I lived through the second dose, no living thing would ever survive on my body.

Coming back to the present, we arrived in Melbourne after a "hard day's night." (Two nights actually, if you count the one that went missing at the International Date Line). Apparently, after so many years, the authorities had given up trying to keep foreign bugs out of Australia. We left the plane without sanitization.

After meeting Ron Wesner, our tour director, we were transported to the Langham Hotel, conveniently located on the Southbank of the Yarra River and close to downtown. It was listed as a five-star hotel, but I deducted one star when I encountered the odd configuration of floors. We entered on the ground floor, which for some reason is not designated as the *first* floor, rode an escalator up past the first and second floors, to the third floor where a check-in counter, tour desk, and concierge reside.

Soon after we checked in, we left for a river cruise on the Yarra River. We boarded the *Yarra Empress*, picked up our name tags, and gathered around Ron, who, in an attempt to set the tone for the trip, read a statement, titled, "Attitude" from a document authored by the Reverend Mr. Swindol:

> The longer I live, the more I realize the impact of attitude on life…The remarkable thing is we have a choice every day regarding the attitude we will embrace for that day…I am convinced that life is 10% what happens to me, and 90% how I react to it. And so it is with you…we are in charge of our Attitudes.

I thought the message was a little repressive, but maybe I was suffering from the "tall poppy syndrome" (a term primarily used in the UK, Australia, and New Zealand, in which people of genuine merit are resented)—or that somehow my naughty boy reputation had preceded my arrival.

The boat was equipped with large viewing windows, dining accommodations, flexible food and beverage menus, and bar tabs, which most of us took advantage of—because we weren't on board for the food.

While the windows were clean, they were curved and reflective; not beneficial to photo ops. To take clear pictures, I joined other photo buffs at the tiny, open space on the stern. It was so crowded, it was a wonder we didn't lift the bow out of the water.

The cruise gave us a riverside look at various commercial buildings, including sporting venues and a casino that like all Australian gambling establishments, provided "pokies" (poker machines), and the second tallest all-residential building in the world at ninety-one floors. It was all black with horizontal white strips at the numerous balconies and so narrow it looked like a closed zipper.

As we cruised on, Southgate Precinct, a dining, shopping, and entertainment destination, spread out before us. Sandwiched between the Crown Casino complex and the Art Centre, this complex has something for everyone, including the Off Ya Tree, alternative store.

"There," Ron said. "You can get Goth and rock shirts, posters, band merchandise, naughty magazines, bongs, paraphernalia for every sort of piercing, and piercing is available as well."

I wasn't interested. I had enough of *alternative cultures* when I had tried to teach high school English to the hippie generation.

Southgate is also home to some of Melbourne's most popular restaurants, bars, and cafes. Food choices range from takeaway food court fare to fine dining options—though most cover the range in between.

Later, we drifted by the Sea Life Melbourne Aquarium. Ron said, "The stunning Croc Lair exhibit is just one of the zones of discovery at the aquarium. You can also marvel at the world's only Elephant Shark display. They are found only in the shallow waters of the Melbourne Peninsula."

I said, "It sounds like some kind of miscarriage of nature. Does it have a trunk or what?"

Ron said, "Elephant Sharks can be easily recognized by the hoe-shaped structure on their snout. This unique species uses their distinctive nose like a metal detector to search the sea floor for shellfish."

We disembarked near the Docklands, another area that offers a colorful variety of events and attractions including a library, sports court, community garden, and over forty-five public artworks.

Back at the hotel, we dressed for dinner—the latest tourist chic—and left to board the burgundy colored Colonial Tramcar Restaurant, an 1891 bistro on wheels. It reminded me of the Pacific Electric Red Car that I used to ride to the Long Beach Pike on days when I skipped high school.

The tramcar was outfitted in red velvet with brass trimmings, like vintage European Pullman-style trains, but with modern amenities such as climate control, one-way windows, onboard music, and a maître d' who led us to our embellished table where we surveyed a little piece of Queen Victoria's history while we were pampered by professional silver-service waiters.

While rolling along on dedicated trolley lines throughout the city we scanned the scenic streets of Melbourne. As we ate, the trolley sometimes moved forward and sometimes backward, but it made no difference to our appetite.

This experience was our first introduction to four course meals (most included in the cost of the tour, thank God). I encountered such appetizers as chicken liver and cognac pâté crowned with a port wine and pink peppercorns; entrees that included Kangaroo loin brushed with lemon myrtle, thyme and honey, served on a vegetable and chive frittata with bush tomato chili jam; a main course included grilled chicken fillet served on a Mediterranean vegetable risotto with pesto, shaved parmesan and a roasted tomato sauce. To finish off, we had a choice of desserts: Warm sticky date pudding topped with butterscotch sauce served with cream or white chocolate and passion fruit parfait with praline and vanilla raspberry syrup. All of this while downing selected Victorian red and white wine, followed by coffee and a wee dram of Cognac.

Because I like my food "naked," I had a hard time ordering, let alone deciphering all of the menu options, but what I ended up with was tasty. However, I had no problem with the spirits—I wasn't driving.

The next morning, we took a bus tour through the city. In the residential areas, two-story houses, sporting wrought iron balcony grillwork, intermingled with long, narrow, one-story houses. The scene reminded me of Bourbon Street in the "Quarter" and the "shotgun" dwellings in suburban New Orleans.

Shopping areas stretched out in long blocks, like Oxford Street in London, filled with stores rather than malls. In one section of town, I noticed a store front sign that read, "Ladies for Gentlemen," which advertised a legal brothel with discrete parking in the rear. Reconstruction occurred in another area, which at one time sustained an old bath house. Ron said, "Legend has it that the freshest water was available on the top level and to bathe at that level you had to pay extra. Lord knows what the water was like at the bottom level."

The bathhouse lineup reminded me of the bathing routine I encountered when I stayed with an uncle and his family on their Montana farm. We had no running water, so it was pumped into buckets that were placed on a stove. The heated water was then poured into an elliptical, tin bathtub. Then, the fun began. The bathing order was established, first my aunt, then my uncle followed by my two cousins, and finally me. As each relative finished, the water was left in the tub. After each subsequent person settled into the murky water, more hot water was added. By the time it was my turn, the water was far less than clear; sometimes it was really dirty. I was faced with a dilemma—would I be cleaner *with* a bath or cleaner *without* one?

Several times, the bus was involved with the infamous Melbourne Hook—the wackiest right turn anywhere. (Keep in mind that Australians drive on the left side of the road.) Because trolleys travel in the middle of the street, and vehicles are not allowed to block their way, drivers who wish to make a right turn must pull over to the left curb as far as possible from where they want to be…sit there for an indeterminate period, until just before the light changes—then, before the cross traffic runs into them, expedite their right turn. The "hook" is often as confusing as my explanation.

As we continued traveling, Ron entertained us with stories of some of the famous Melbourne personalities, including Nellie Melba and Ned Kelly:

Ron said, "Vocalist Nellie Melba rose from childhood in provincial Australia to become a world-renowned opera soprano who performed regularly at London's Covent Garden and the Metropolitan Opera in New York. In her day, the sometimes-outlandish, seemingly larger-than-life Melba was famed around the globe for her beautiful singing and her commanding stage presence. She helped popularize opera throughout Europe and the United States in an era where opera stars not only hobnobbed with royalty, but were often treated like royalty themselves. And no one demanded royal treatment more insistently than Melba. She was so well known her name became attached to several popular foods named in her honor: Melba toast and the dessert, Peach Melba.

Ned Kelly is an Australian legend. He epitomized many qualities that ordinary Australians admire. He was loyal to his family and ready to sacrifice himself for his mates. An underdog, he represented the struggling classes and thumbed his nose at the establishment. He was inventive, he was fearless, and charismatic. He killed police officers, committed bank robberies, and could be shot on sight by anyone. Yet, when he was sentenced to hang, more than 30,000 people signed a petition asking for a reprieve. It's claimed that most of the takings from his famous bank robberies went to help his supporters; so, many say Ned was an Australian Robin Hood. Journalist Martin Flanagan writes, "What makes Ned a legend is not that everyone sees him the same—it's that everyone sees him. Like a bushfire on the horizon casting its red glow into the night."

We made our way to the Shrine of Remembrance, a memorial to all Australians who served in war. There, we gathered at the World War II forecourt near a tall granite pillar inscribed with the names of the defense forces, together with the theatres of war they served in. Atop the monument, rests a basalt sculpture of six servicemen carrying a bier with a corpse, draped by the Australian flag. Representing eternal life, the Eternal Flame reaches up nearby.

Ron told us that the original shrine was constructed to honor the sacrifice Australians made to commemorate the tragedy that occurred in Gallipoli, Turkey, during WWI, but as time and wars moved on, the monument was expanded to cover all conflicts in which Australians took part.

The shrine is constructed in the classical style like the Parthenon in Athens, Greece. The east and west facing fronts are marked at the corners by four groups of statuary representing Peace, Justice, Patriotism, and Sacrifice.

At the center of the sanctuary, the Stone of Remembrance is recessed, requiring visitors to bow their heads to read the inscription, "GREATER LOVE HATH NO MAN…." Beneath the sanctuary lies a crypt, which contains a bronze statue of a soldier father and son, and panels listing every unit of the Australian Imperial Force.

As I wandered about observing fateful memorabilia, the strains of, "And the Band Played Waltzing Matilda" drifted throughout the vaulted hall. The song is an account of the memories of an old Australian man who, in 1915, had been recruited into the Australian and New

Zealand Army Corps and sent to Gallipoli. For "ten weary weeks, he kept himself alive as around the corpses piled higher." He recalls "that terrible day…in the hell that they called Suvla Bay [they] were butchered like lambs at the slaughter ... in that mad world of blood, death and fire." He is ultimately hit by a shell and awakens in the hospital to learn that he has lost both his legs.

When the ship carrying the young soldiers departs from Australia the band plays Waltzing Matilda while crowds wave flags and cheer. However when the crippled narrator returns and "the legless, the armless, the blind, the insane" are carried down the gangway to the same popular music, the crowd watches in silence and turn their faces away.

As I listened to the song and looked around, I was emotionally overwhelmed. Tears followed, as my thoughts turned to Marine Corps buddies who lost their lives or were maimed in Korea.

We departed our bus tour at the Altman Cherney opal establishment in the downtown district, the center of the opal trade. A salesman, eager to show us around, opened a huge safe that displayed the largest opal in the world. I was impressed. Then, we watched a video that illustrated opal farming and the four grades of opals. Afterward, we were led to the "slaughter" (the display cases). All of the jewelry was beyond my pay grade, even those pieces discounted at fifty percent off.

Since I didn't want to max out my credit card on my second day out, I convinced Sharon that we might find a better deal elsewhere. No such luck. The prices were the same in every opal shop that we visited. No sign of collusion there, right?

The streets of the shopping district were crowded, and there seemed to be no rule as to how to pass oncoming pedestrians, so we encountered a lot of walking into each other. I tired of this game early on, so I took to placing my large camera in front of my stomach to jab oblivious strollers who got too close.

We stopped for coffee inside the nineteenth century Queen Victoria Market, the largest open air market in the Southern Hemisphere. The Market offers a variety of foods as well as specialty delicacies. It also has a large non-food related section.

It was our first experience ordering coffee in Australia. I read the menu above and behind the counter of the small coffee bar. Listed, were the usual espresso delights—cappuccinos, lattes, mochas, and macchiatos. Also listed were the designations, "short black, long black, flat white," and "Americano."

I asked the counter-person, what the last four designations meant.

He said, "All are made with espresso coffee. Short black has no water added: long black is a tall cup in which hot water is poured first then the espresso; flat white, is made with steamed milk; and Americano has same ingredients as long black, but with an opposite pouring sequence."

I said, "Two short Americanos, please."

"They will have to be tall."

"Can't you put the mix in a small cup?"

"No, it wouldn't be proper. Besides that designation is not listed on our computer."

"Can't you lie to the computer, and prepare the coffee as requested?"

"No, the mix would not be correct. You probably would not like it."

Seeing that I was pursuing a lost cause, I said, "Okay, make it two tall Americanos."

One thing to note is that regular drip coffee is hard to find. You'll have to switch to short black or long black, and they do not have Half and Half, or cream for that matter at cafes, just milk.

I paid the check with a twenty Australian dollar bill. No pennies exist in Australia and prices are exact without adding sales tax. Everything comes out even or is rounded off to the next five cents. It was nice to get change that counts such as the dollar and two-dollar coins, even though for some strange reason, the two-dollar coin is much smaller than the one-dollar coin.

After more shopping—mostly the window kind—we broke for lunch at the Elephant and Wheelbarrow Pub. This name, a carryover of funny pub names from Britain, must have had significance for its originator, but not to anyone in the pub that day. We had plain fish and chips, what else? What a treat to eat recognizable food, but because it was an English pub, not Irish, my favorite beer, Harp, was unavailable.

Later, several of our group went looking for the famous Australian Akubra hat that is the trademark of the Australian look. It's made of the fur from seven rabbit skins (whose counting), and is one of the best ways to keep the sun off your noggin (Australia is considered the skin cancer capital of the world). Because the hat is made from rabbit fur, and because Australia is practically overrun with rabbits, the process serves two purposes, a serviceable attractive dome cover and a way to rid the country of a pest. Luckily, PETA doesn't have a chapter there.

Sharon and I were left to "walkabout" on our own. Our first stop was at a store where Sharon purchased a pair of opaque, wrap around sunglasses.

Sharon said, "My lot in life is always facing the sun, get sun sneezes, become totally blind, and grabbing on to poor you as I swerve along. Australia has monstrous sun! Imagine my delight in finding a pair of Australian sunglasses. They are not flattering. I'm sure that I will be blind as a bat wearing them back home, and I will get some funny looks, but what a find."

Next, we went to the post office to get stamps for postcards. I wasn't ready for the long line. People pay their utility bills there. One guy, probably just ahead of arrest for non-payment, must have shelled out $1,000 for assorted debts.

Finally, we retired to a restaurant called Pure South along the river walk, near our hotel.

We sat outside and ordered drinks. Sharon had her usual martini and I had an "unusual" margarita—the drink tasted like lemonade sans booze. For my second drink, I introduced the bartender to the Cadillac margarita, asking him to add some tequila and Grand

Marnier liqueur to the lemonade, and later he introduced me to the high cost of cocktails in Australia—$32 for two drinks. We sat there for two hours (a period of hush and wonderment, as Sharon calls it). It was a great spot to watch people and we played a game of trying to identify tourists and locals. It was too easy, tourists were those who wore sunglasses and/or strange hats and were usually overweight.

Sharon said, "Have you been here before?"

To be funny, I said, "In this particular restaurant or in Melbourne?"

She said. "In Melbourne, Silly."

"On a previous trip we arrived in Melbourne on a Friday, and booked a side trip to Phillip Island to see the Fairy penguins—they are the smallest of the species.

"Don't you mean Phillip's Island?"

"No, the Australians named the island after Arthur Phillip, the first Governor of New South Wales, without being possessive about it."

"Another of your many puns?"

"Yep! Anyway, when we got to the hotel, we were told that no tours went out to see the Fairy penguins on Fridays, and we were out of luck. However, the tour bus driver, a kind-hearted soul, said he would drive us out to the site for forty Australian dollars each. Evidently, his heart didn't reach out to his wallet. It was a stiff price, but we didn't want to miss the opportunity.

After dark, as we boarded the bus, the driver went back into the hotel and returned with blankets. He said it would be cold out on the island so we needed to bundle up.

"We drove about fifty miles to stand in the rain and sleet to see the little critters come ashore. It was 'colder than a witch's tit' below forty degrees Fahrenheit and dropping, and it was dark as doom, but the moon appeared here and there just enough to make out the breakers and the beach. It wasn't too long before I could see the shapes of the little birds swimming toward shore. They surfed as far as their bellies would let them; then they stood up and waddled toward a fenced off area that enclosed their underground nests, and disappeared."

Sharon said, "Was it worth it?"

I said, "You bet."

With that exchange, we were ready to order something to eat. However we soon discovered that we were looking at another four course menu, including Wessex Saddleback Pork, fattened premium Flinders Island Lamb, Springfield Farm venison, rare Tasmanian Black Perigord Truffles, oysters from Coles Bay, and abalone and black mussels and scallops from the boats on the East Coast of Tasmania. After we added an expensive meal—a Tasmanian Cheese Plate, $19—to our check, we returned to our hotel to prepare for our departure on the "morrow."

Chapter 2

In and Outback

After our arrival in Alice Springs, with Roger at the wheel of our bus, Ron spoke of the racial issues regarding the Aboriginals and white Australians; of South Australian Superintendent of Telegraphs, Charles Todd, who strung the "singing line" across the continent; and of his wife, Alice, who gave her name to Alice Springs. Actually, the township of Alice Springs takes its name from a waterhole a short distance east of the Telegraph Station, but, of course, that application is less romantic.

Our visit to Alice's name sake was brief to say the least, just a look at two historical sites, and a restroom adorned with meaningful graffiti: "The world is full of apathy, but who gives a crap"; and "Fly the Flag," which I found out later meant "wear a condom." Then, it was back on the plane for the flight to Ayers Rock.

Our first encounter with times-gone-by occurred at the Royal Flying Doctor Service established in 1928 by Reverend John Flynn. Using air links and radio, the service provided medical aid to people living, working, and travelling in the outback. Today it operates twenty-one bases and covers more than 2,780,000 square miles.

In Alice Springs, what started as a small medical office has blossomed into the current visitor's mecca. I entered a full-size replica of a modern PC 12 airplane, but skipped the rest of the exhibits, including touch screen portals that provide insight into the lives of RFDS personnel, a seventy-seat theatre, a café, and the "Doc Shop," a retail store that sells a wide range of tourist fodder. Since I had purchased a shot glass on a previous visit, I relaxed on a bench while Sharon perused the knickknacks.

Our second stop, the Alice Springs Telegraph Station Historical Reserve, built in 1872 to relay messages between Darwin and Adelaide, is the best preserved of the twelve stations along the Overland Telegraph Line.

After sixty years of operation, the premises served as a school for the local Aboriginal children. Now it functions as a historical reserve featuring the original stone buildings and furnishings from the early 1900s.

In the Post and Telegraph Room, while you are prevented from accessing the original equipment, you can still post a letter and send a telegram (email) to a loved one or friend.

In the cooler months of May through October, the wood-fired oven is lit and "damper" (outback bread) and scones are served. We were too early (or too late) for this celebration, but I hungered for the bread and scones, without the heat from the oven. It must have been 110 degrees in the shade the day we visited.

On our way back to the airport, I caught a glimpse of one of the world's largest vehicles—the road train, which is a combination of a huge three axle tractor pulling three trailers (triples), loaded to the "gunnels" with all manner of cargo, including livestock, fuel, automobiles, and general freight.

The road train is the only way to transport goods across the outback, which is larger than some European countries, and encompasses more than 100,000 square miles of empty, arid, and beastly hot wasteland, where only a few brave souls dare to live in small communities totally reliant on road train deliveries.

When we landed at the small Ayers Rock airport, we had to schlep our own luggage to the bus, no porters or carts were available. We then rode to the well-dressed Sails in the Desert, so named because the hotel forecourt is built like a sailing ship where tri-cornered canvas "sails" attach to mast-like poles and stretch out horizontally overhead providing shade for a large patio and the entrance to the lobby.

At 4:30 p.m., we drove to Uluru–Kata Tjuta National Park. In the distance, Uluru (Ayers Rock) rose abruptly from the scrubland. One of Australia's most recognizable natural landmarks, Uluru looms 1,150 feet above the flat desert landscape, and is about 2.2 miles long, 1.2 miles wide and over five miles in circumference. Since there is nothing of any size or relation to the rock anywhere near it or even on the horizon, it appears to have been plopped down, like a massive glob of red clay, by some ancestral beings.

Both Uluru and the nearby Kata Tjuta formation have great cultural significance for the Anangu—a label that originally meant "human being"—but has come to refer to Aboriginals, the traditional inhabitants of the area. Some Aboriginals lead walking tours to inform visitors about the local flora and fauna, bush foods, and the Australian Aboriginal Dreamtime, a concept of "time out of time," or "everywhen" inhabited by ancestral figures, often heroic. These stories are recorded in the fissures, cliffs, and caves of the rock itself.

Accordingly, one myth relates to creation:

> The world was once a featureless place. None of the places we know existed until creator beings, in the forms of people, plants and animals, traveled widely across the land. Then, in a process of creation and destruction, they formed the landscape, as we know it today. Anangu land is still inhabited by the spirits of dozens of these ancestral creator beings, which are referred to as Tjukuritja or Waparitja. (Don't ask me how to pronounce either one.)

Another legend relates to the rock itself:

> Two tribes of ancestral spirits were invited to a feast in the area, but became distracted by beautiful Sleepy Lizard Women and dallied at a waterhole. Angry at being stood up, the waiting hosts sang evil into a mud sculpture that came to life as the dingo, a wild dog that has been known to carry off babies. There was a terrible slaughter followed by a great battle, which ended in the deaths of the leaders of both tribes. The earth itself rose up in grief at the bloodshed—and this is Uluru.

At the beginning of our tour of Uluru, I was reluctant to cover my face with a fly net attached to a wide brimmed hat (not the most fashionable accessory), but quickly realized my mistake. Hundreds of the most persistent flies in the world, tried to suck moisture off of anything; especially from the backs of my hands, my face, ears, nose, and even my tongue if I didn't keep my mouth shut. They wouldn't give up, even in the throes of death. If one landed on me and stayed a second or two, it was like an invitation for hundreds of relatives to join in the fun. At first, I practiced the "outback salute,"—an open hand swished across my face—but finally donned my hat-net. It was either that or slap myself silly.

One woman on the tour began to smash the flies on the back of her hand, not realizing that the blood and guts that gathered on her skin attracted even more suicidal flies. I apprised her of that fact, but she continued to smudge them all to death.

Uluru is completely bare, without the least bit of vegetation. By contrast, however, the base of the rock, sustained by very little rain runoff, is rife with small pools of water and greenery.

With netting in place, and pocketed hands, I could enjoy the tour. Thankfully, the guide selected specific areas to look at, instead of the five-mile hike around the perimeter.

We looked into shallow caves at the base of the monolith, which contain ancient carvings and paintings. But unlike other static cave art sites, they are still being created by the Anangu. The old cave drawings are simply painted over with new ones, including figures such as boomerangs, human beings, waterholes and abstract symbols—so abstract and overlaid, in fact, it is impossible to tell what's what. However, I'm sure they make sense to someone, the guides in particular.

Then, it was on to the still-in-use Mutu Tjulu Waterhole. On the way we were entertained with a natural history lesson of the geology and the flora of the surroundings. We came across flies, rock paintings, flies, burnt gum trees, flies, heat, and more flies.

We turned a corner (if rocks have corners), and found ourselves at the entrance to the rock climb, the traditional path up to the summit of the rock taken by aboriginal ancestors upon their arrival at Uluru in the creation time.

Because of its sacredness, the Anangu don't climb Uluru, and a sign at the base of Uluru posted by the Aborigines specifically requests visitors not to climb their sanctified rock.

However, since Uluru is currently leased to Australia as a national park, and despite being discouraged by its traditional owners, some visitors still climb the "island mountain."

Even though the path is marked with chain handholds to make it a little safer, the steep, half-mile hike to the top is no easy task and some risk-takers have even died in the attempt.

Climbing Uluru is generally closed to the public when high winds are present at the top. Other closures have occurred because of acts of crest (or crestfallen) stupidity, such as people tee-ing off golf balls, stripping for photos, and frolicking nude in a back-to-nature kind of way.

The trail was thankfully closed when we arrived at the entrance, otherwise some of the more foolish in our group, me included, would have tried the ascent. However, disappointment led to pleasure after we drove to a large area to picnic and watch Uluru change colors at sunset.

While we enjoyed Champaign and beer—but not together—and canapés, of which I had none, the sun slowly set on the horizon creating a panorama of color on Uluru, from sunshine enriched light brown to the deep, rusty red color that glows just before dark.

I was glad we had reservations in a designated shady spot because the air had gone from warm to hot, was frying my arse, and the place was crowded! Almost 5,000 people visit Uluru per week. Can you believe it? Out there in the middle of nowhere!

On our way back to Sails in the Desert, I reminisced about a previous trip to Ayers Rock:

> Light rain fell, a leftover from a tremendous thunder burst moments before. Scores of tiny waterfalls cascaded down all sides of the rock. At one cradle in the rock, a large cataract rushed over the depression, the water forming reflective ponds below so clear the trees and shrubs nearby mirrored in the pools. High up on one side of the rock, dark cavities, which looked like joints in a spinal column, spilled water in succession downward. Enshrined in mist, the

top of the rock vanished. What was visible below the vapor was no longer beautiful. The warm rock colors, lacking enhancing sunshine, morphed into several shades of gray.

It almost never rains at Ayers Rock, so I was privy to a phenomenon that is rarely seen. Had I not lived up to the Boy Scout motto, "Be Prepared," I would have surely been soaked. Needless to say, the plastic rain slicker I had brought along on the trip was ill fitting at best, but it served its purpose.

Chapter 3

Absurdities and
Flights of Fancy

Our return to Alice Springs was a surprise to all of us except Ron, our tour guide. It seemed like we were wasting time backtracking.

I asked Ron, "Why this convoluted arrangement?"

He said, "We couldn't get rooms at the booked hotel for a longer stay, so we made arrangements at a different hotel. Rooms were available, but not for a couple of days, so that's why we are going back."

I said, "Thanks, that makes sense, but somebody screwed up."

"Well, it wasn't me."

To sweeten the pot, Tauck Tours provided a private airplane for our small group of thirty-nine pilgrims. This was our first flight, but not the last on the Convair "prop job."

It was nice not to have to contend with hundreds of other passengers, except it was a chore to drag our luggage for some distance to the plane, and then to haul carry-ons up the steps, and through the doorway. The steps seemed to lengthen, and the luggage seemed to increase in weight each time we boarded the aircraft.

It was a short flight to Alice Springs. After checking into the hotel, which was less attractive than a "hot-sheet" motel, we walked through a tunnel-like causeway to find the stairs (no elevator) to our drab, upper level room.

Later we bussed to a dreamtime station near an Aboriginal camp to meet with Mark Stewart who gave us insights into the Aboriginal culture and their stories of creation put into songs—the only way their language remains constant. They have no written language, simply an oral language that changes over time. Even their paintings are subject to interpretation.

On a previous trip, I was apprised of the Aboriginal oral tradition and how well it adapted to the English language:

> While waiting for shoppers, I sat alone in a small bus parked in front of a store. Because it was hot, both the front and rear doors were open for ventilation. As I looked through the rear opening, I noticed an Aboriginal standing by the side of the building. When he saw the tourist bus with me inside, he let out a stream of English expletives interspersed with his favorite, "fuck you." He was well versed in scatology but little else. When the diatribe ended, he displayed his skill in sign language— with his left hand grabbing his bicep, he thrust his forearm skyward accompanied with a closed fist except for the middle finger "wave." Obviously, he had no love for Italian or American tourists.

When the lecture was over, Ron, getting into the spirit, ate a witchetty grub (a large, white, wood-eating larvae of the cossid moth), and two other guys did the same. They all said the larva tasted like fresh corn. When they offered one of the wiggling insect to me, I respectfully declined.

After the disgusting grub-crunching demonstration, we enjoyed a *corroboree*, an Australian Aboriginal dance ceremony. The all-male (shucks) Dreamtime dancers were dressed, or *undressed*—in their finest loincloth, which barely covered their "possibles," and adorned with headbands, emu feathers, shell pendants and necklaces, nose bones, and white body paint. Some, holding shields, spears, and clubs, "shuffled off to Buffalo," while musicians of a sort played the didgeridoo and other home-made instruments I had never seen—or heard—before. The sound was a little short of harmony.

Less than a dreamtime adventure, lunch followed. We had to eat under large, tent-like, white netting that covered us and a few flies that had managed to crash the party. Whenever a server or diner lifted an edge of the netting to enter or leave, the fly population grew until it was almost impossible to lift my facial netting to eat—*rapidly*, I might add. A couple of times when I forgot to lift my personal fly protection, I found out that it was impossible to eat "bush tucker" through mesh. Sharon and others had the same problem, which created a laughing fit.

After lunch, we walked over to an area where some brave artists who were willing to challenge the oppressive heat and the ubiquitous, unabated flies displayed authentic Aboriginal paintings.

Some in our group bought paintings and had their picture taken with the artists who made the buyers look good. Others were brave enough to try the culinary delight of the outback—grubs.

Later, we visited Alice Springs Desert Park, a recreated desert in the desert (go figure). Sharon and I started our stroll well enough, but soon we began to skip many of the displays of plants and animals, and other secrets of the desert, which were no longer a secret to Sharon and me since we live on a high desert plain. It was too "shagging" hot. Of course, it was a dry heat according to the locals, but my sweat glands didn't get the word.

We quickly headed for salvation from the heat—to the Nocturnal House, snack bar and, as always, a gift shop, all air conditioned.

At the large Nocturnal House, where all manner of night creatures lived enclosed behind glass panels, with such poor light, the animals and birds were rendered practically invisible. With so little to see, excitement occurred mostly at times when I walked into walls, partitions, and other searchers.

At a prescribed time, we entered a theater to watch a multimedia presentation of the Dreamtime: a concept of "time out of time," or "everywhen," inhabited by ancestral figures, often of heroic proportions or with supernatural abilities—but not considered "gods" as they do not control the material world and are not worshipped. However, by the time I began to understand the symbols, language, and purpose, the drama was over.

And then it was back to the inferno outside to see a somewhat limited but exciting birds of prey show: A black kite, a hawk, and then a bashful small gray falcon. It refused to participate until the audience was leaving, then at the last minute performed admirably; flying free and grabbing food in midair.

Two of Alice Springs most popular attractions are the world's weirdest boat race, the Henley-on-Todd Regatta, and the iconic Australian saloon, Bojangles.

Every year, around September, the town holds the boat race, a parody of the more traditional rowing races between crews representing the University of Oxford and the University of Cambridge that takes place on the River Thames at Henley, England. Food and drink are sold at stalls, "no fishing" signs are put up, and the celebration continues all day.

To enhance the spoof, the race occurs only if there is *no* water in the Todd River. It is the only regatta ever cancelled because of wet weather. In addition, the "boats," made from metal frames and hung with banners and advertisements, lack bottoms. Teams of "rowers" run along inside the bottomless boats, through the hot sand, while holding on to the sides.

Races are also held in washtubs, human-sized hamster wheels, and at the final event, modified trucks decked out as boats driven by costumed teams armed with flour bombs and water cannons. Since announcers and many bystanders end up as casualties of the final battle, and the pandemonium is so intense, determining the winner is often up for grabs.

We were, again, too early (or too late) for the hilarity, but not for Bojangles Saloon and Restaurant. The walls were adorned with a wild assortment of memorabilia, such as a real motorcycle, a homemade suit of armor, and historical photos. A seventeen foot crocodile, "a bloody big lizard," stretches out above one bar and Reggie, a wedge tailed eagle with wide spread wings, hovers above another. A life sized replica of the notorious bandit, Ned Kelly, guards the bat wing front doors, and a live eight foot python was supposed to be "hanging" around somewhere, but no one could find him.

While talking to bartender Max Cameron, a Māori from Rotorua, New Zealand, I said, "I was here twenty years ago."

Max said, "What's your last name?"

"Williams," I said.

With that, he turned around and walked through a door behind the bar. When he came back he presented me with the following note:

If a Mister Herb Williams comes in he needs to pay his bill 20 years ago:
> **Stage coach to Alice, £20 British pounds**
> **Beer account, £60;**
> **Lady of the night, 200 pounds (money not weight).**
> **Converted today, including interest, to 50 thousand US dollars.**

Max added, "The lady of the night is my grandmother and is in a wheelchair and needs the money."

Naturally, I denied all of the charges, but I bought him a beer.

The restaurant serves true territory tucker (native animal fare) such as camel, croc, kangaroo, emu, and barramundi (certainly not from the Todd River), and the "Big Bugger," a 600 gram, T-bone steak, the size of Ayers Rock.

I declined all and satiated myself with a bar stool sized hamburger made with beef, cheese, bacon, fried eggs, onions, and mushrooms, garnished with lettuce, tomato, mustard, and some kind of secret sauce. I struggled to finish the burger, but I managed to wash it down with a couple of beers. Needless to say, I waddled back to the hotel.

Early the next morning (at 4:45 a.m.), we rode into total darkness (there are no street lights in the Australian outback) to find two hot air balloons in which we were to sail through the sky. When we arrived at the site, the bus lights, accompanied by a couple of battery operated floodlights, were all that held back the blackness. The illuminated space revealed little more than wicker baskets (gondolas) lying on their sides, stretched out ropes attached to the basket with carabiners (spring hooks), and the bottom edges of the balloons.

The balloon, or envelop, nearest me was stretched out well beyond the pale, probably over a hundred yards at least, into the void. Way out in the gloom, I heard the faint call, "Inflate the bag."

Placed between the envelope and the gondola, a huge gasoline powered fan whirred into action, blowing cold air into the mouth of the balloon to partially inflate it. The earsplitting noise shattered the quiet desert air.

After the basic shape of the balloon was established, the fan was shut off. Then, tank-fed, wide open twin burners, attached to rigging at the top of the basket, whooshed alive as huge flames leaped toward the expanding inflatable.

As the hot air rushed into the lifting envelope, a crew member held a rope tied to the crown to prevent it from excessive sway—and from rising before it was sufficiently buoyant.

Sunrise, an orange glow, diffused by striated purple clouds, revealed the largest gondola and balloon I have ever seen. Fully inflated, the envelope stood as tall as a twelve-story building. Anxious to be aloft, it up righted the attached gondola, which was large enough to carry eighteen passengers and the pilot.

I stood watching the evolution of the monstrosity while finishing a less than nourishing breakfast of juice, cheese, crackers, and a huge drumstick, which I declined to eat. I thought the "delicacy" looked more like a roadrunner's appendage than a chicken's leg.

Once the balloon was upright, the pilot climbed into the gondola and motioned for us "fledglings" to join him.

To get inside of the basket, we had to climb over the four-foot edge. I barely made it, I got one leg in but my other leg hung up on the rim at such a stretch, I could not lift it over. Finally, a handsome, buffed out "mate" lifted my uncooperative leg and dropped it inside. Sharon, after considerable worry about how she was going to climb into the gondola, was lifted in by the same guy. She was ecstatic.

Fully loaded, sixteen of us stood in partitioned rows, four in each row, eight to a side.

Sharon said, "I don't want to stand too close to the edge of the basket."

I said, "Well you have two options. If you stand in the middle, you will roast. If you stand as close to the farthest edge as possible, you will be cooler but fearful."

"Do the burners really create that much heat?"

"Yep. I suggest you stand as far away from them as possible."

She followed my instructions and joined me at the rim of the gondola. I held her close to relieve her anxiety.

Then, it was time to launch. The pilot turned up the flame. The heat intensified, and the balloon, and gondola of course, ascended into the lightening sky.

Sharon relaxed and even peered over the edge of the gondola, but not for long. She expressed her gratitude for suggesting she stand as far away from the burners as possible. Even then, she pulled her wide-brimmed hat down on the back of her head for more protection from the heat. With my own hat, I followed her example. I looked like a cowboy with a high forehead.

Except for the periodic hiss of the burners, we silently drifted over a large swath of the terrain looking for wildlife and enjoying a beautiful sunrise. Nothing was stirring except for some four-legged kangaroos (cows).

A little while after we adjusted to the silence and the loftiness, the pilot opened the vent at the top of the balloon to let hot air escape, decreasing the temperature inside it—and outside of us as well, which reduced lift in preparation for landing.

I could see the chase vehicles waiting for us at the desired landing spot, a narrow, country road.

The basket bumped the asphalt a couple of times, but settled shortly. After the balloon was anchored I, and all other passengers disembarked, except for Sharon. She waited for help to lift her out of the basket, hoping, I'm sure, for the handsome, buffed out dude to offer his services. She wasn't disappointed. He put one arm under her thighs, wrapped the other arm around her back, and effortlessly lifted her out of the contraption.

Later, in the bush, we had a champagne brunch with chicken, quiche, chocolate cake, coffee and orange juice. Then, we rushed off to the hotel and airport for our flight to Cairns.

Chapter 4

Beauty and Beasts

In Alice Springs, the plane, a twin engine prop job, developed a problem half way into the takeoff, so we had to return to the staging area. We disembarked with our carry-ons, which by now were becoming carry-offs, and returned to the terminal. After four hours of snacking and fitful dozing, we took off for Cairns in a different plane, which carried insufficient fuel for some strange reason. The pilot blamed it on heat expansion.

Sharon suffers from inner-ear pain when departing or landing in the big jets, which was worse in the small non-pressurized substitute. To help relieve the pain, the hostess offered a eucalyptus inhaler to my honey. It did the trick.

Because of the fuel foul-up, we had to land to "top off the tank" in Mt. Isa, a non-descript mining 'burg, where we once again had the "lovely" experience of airport ennui. I couldn't even drink away hours of frustration—the bar was closed.

In retrospect, the long delay was a good thing, since if we had taken off earlier, we would have found ourselves in a terrible storm.

At 10:00 p.m., we landed in Cairns, boarded our coach, and traveled up the Captain Cook Highway. The very scenic asphalted road winds alongside the coast between the reef and rainforest of tropical Queensland, forty-seven miles from Cairns to Mossman. According to the pundits, its ocean views and mountain background make it one of the best drives in the country.

I couldn't vouch for any of the scenery because it was like driving through a black hole in space. To add insult to injury, Sharon and I had finally rotated to the front seat of the bus, the best viewing location, but all we saw was what the lights of the bus revealed—miles of asphalt and overhanging foliage. Sadly, we would never again reach the front view pinnacle.

After midnight, we arrived at Silky Oaks Lodge, and were given our room assignments, keys and a guide to lead us to individual tree houses. We stumbled along in the blackness. I could barely see the guide, let alone the pathway. Finally, in the crocodile cluster (cabanas not predators), we climbed a few steps to enter our bungalow. I opened the door to a beautiful, bright interior, walked across a shiny multi-colored hardwood floor, and was blown away by a large, inviting bed, a marble bathroom with a walk-in rain shower and large corner double spa-bath. Placed on a highly polished, wooden table, a four course meal (sandwiches, chips, fruit, and juice), *au lieu de dinner*, beckoned us to eat.

The next morning I awoke to sunlight filtering through wooden window blinds, and a slight breeze created by an overhead fan. Stepping to a window, I opened the slats and peered out into a tropical rainforest. Then, I opened the door and stepped out onto a large balcony. Looking around I realized we were lodged in an individually placed tree house set high on stilts surrounded by a lush combination of giant ferns, bamboo, and palm and hardwood trees, some I assumed were oaks.

Having filled my senses with the sights and sounds of my surroundings, I relaxed in a wooden chair. An inviting hammock hung nearby, but I chose not to use it. I can get in one, but getting out is impossible for me. I would have needed help from both Sharon and her muscular friend.

The humidity escalated slightly. A harbinger of what the weather was going to be like for the next couple of days. It wasn't really comfortable, but I liked it better than the hot—it's a dry heat—weather in Alice.

Sharon joined me and said, "Isn't this lovely?"

I said, "Yes, it's a jungle paradise. The only thing missing is the Swiss family named Robinson."

Later, we strolled over to a beautiful open sided dining room perched in the midst of the surrounding rainforest and overlooking the sparkling, tranquil waters of the Mossman River. The jungle was dense, but the sun managed to filter through in places, sending flickers into the restaurant and lighting up the web of a large golden orb spider making breakfast out some insect that was unfortunate enough to make the spider's acquaintance. As if to let us know that this area was his domain, the spider had cast his web under the railing next to our table. I was undisturbed, but Sharon was a little queasy and took the chair farthest away from the action.

Down below, scratching for souvenirs, an Australian cassowary was hard at work. To me, it looked like a vulture, which made me think that the bird knew something about the source of the food that I didn't.

While the setting was unique, the breakfast buffet was not. The cook had no idea of what "crisp" meant, so the bacon was limp. The eggs were scrambled soft—the way Sharon likes them. Omelets and fried eggs were usually available as well as a variety of cereals and fruit—my usual traveler's breakfast.

After our repast, it was off to Port Douglas to board the *Quicksilver*, a huge catamaran bound for the Great Barrier Reef, the world's largest coral reef system composed of over 2,900 individual reefs and 900 islands stretching over 1,400 miles covering an area of approximately 133,000 square miles. It's larger than the Great Wall of China and the only *living* thing on Earth visible from space.

Even though free seasickness pills were available, the boat was so big and the captain so reassuring, Sharon chose to forgo the offer. While the trip to the reef was calm as promised, the dialog emanating from the ship's speakers was anything but:

> ...Although jellyfish are regarded as dangerous animals in many parts of the world, most jellyfish are harmless to humans. There are, however, a few species in Australian waters that can kill you, or at least make you very sick. The infamous Australian Box Jellyfish is the most poisonous animal in the world. Another Australian jellyfish that you don't want to befriend is

the 'Hair-Jelly' or 'Snottie,' with a large flat body up to 30cm in diameter, and a 'mop' of hair-like tentacles up to 50cm long.

I was looking forward to arriving at a sun-soaked golden beach, riding on a glass bottom boat, and enjoying an open bar under waving palm trees, as I had on my previous trip. Instead, we moored at an immense floating, ship-like platform that acts as a base for tourists who wish to engage in reef related water sports. The man-made "island," a metal monstrosity of metal decks, metal railings, metal benches, and metal tables and chairs was located in insufficient shade and reserved for diners of meager fare from the nearby snack bar, who then cooked to a melting point. If you weren't hungry, or even if you were, but couldn't stomach what was offered, both gastronomically and economically, you had to roast in the hot sun.

Several barefoot individuals wearing bathing suits were doing a sun dance on the hot aluminum platform waiting for a chance to get into the water. Others had dared to sit too long on one of the metal benches. When they arose, their sunburned backs matched the pattern of the bench's banded metal backrest.

Several water activities were available, but since Australia seems to have a corner on the most deadly varieties of sea life, I was glad I didn't have a bathing suit. I had no desire to be stung or stabbed to death, or eaten alive. And since Sharon and I no longer snorkel, and never dive, we chose to board a semi-submersible, underwater observatory much like the one at Disneyland, but here the reef was real instead of fabricated.

Thirty to forty mariners (tourists) descended into the depths of the "sub." It was a bit claustrophobic for me, but the viewing was so spectacular, I forgot about the closeness. Besides, I knew we weren't totally underwater.

I observed giant clams (some opening for "dinner"), sea slugs slithering easily over rough coral surfaces, starfish clinging to whatever they called home, and many varieties of small multicolored fish, some schooling, others darting individually amongst kaleidoscopic, strangely formed polyps, feathery tentacles, and undulating varieties of sea anemones reaching up to catch a meal. Missing was the marine life that possess a bite or sting that is fatal to humans. However, I thought I saw a "Snottie," so named, I suspect, because it looks like mucus and has a bad attitude.

When we returned to Silky Oaks we enjoyed a barbeque, sans fish, in the elevated restaurant. I was joyous (I could finally get proper food and drink), and sad at the same time. It was miserable to think of leaving this paradise.

The following morning, as we drove through the sugar cane fields, Mike, our driver, told us stories about Queensland and the Coral Sea with emphasis on the naval battle that erupted there early in WWII, of which I was overly familiar. I have watched the movie, *Midway*, a million times. Well, maybe just a couple thousand.

We arrived at Hartley's Creek Crocodile Farm for an exciting visit with Goldie, Bob, and a bunch of other crocs that shall remain nameless.

We boarded a small, flat bottom boat and as we drifted along through Hartley's Lagoon, a man-made wetland supporting a wide range of flora and fauna, our driver and guide took great delight in feeding naked chickens, dead of course, to huge saltwater crocodiles. His favorite was a twelve-foot monster that loafed in the water as if he was unconcerned with the whole chicken dangling from the end of a line attached to a long pole. Suddenly, enough to create jumps and gasps from the boat passengers, the crocodile sprang almost six feet out of the water and snapped at the featherless corpse, only to miss as the attendant pulled it upward. The game was played over and over again until the croc either got tired of it or finally grasped the chicken.

After the third or fourth try, I was bored as well. I liked the entertainment better when on a previous croc hunt; the guide fed a large ball of marshmallows to one of the monsters. The crocodile couldn't chew up the sticky mass and couldn't swallow it, so it continued to move its jaws like someone chewing gum with an open mouth. It was hilarious to watch as the beast kept chomping away, but even though the croc grinned, I could tell he didn't think the prank was funny.

Following the chicken dippin' the guide told stories of these animals leaping from the water from time to time to snatch and devour unsuspecting tourists, and then demonstrated the sexual habits of the reptile using two small, stuffed crocs with tails that could be intertwined. I guess by looking at our older faces, he thought we had forgotten about sex, or that we were hungry for the exotic. Well, it did spice up the trip.

After leaving the crocodile farm, with our new knowledge of croc feeding and sexual habits, we visited Tjapukai (don't ask me how to pronounce this), Aboriginal Park.

At the park, we observed authentic Stone Age artifacts, and witnessed a live rendition of an ancient celebration of song and dance. Dressed, or undressed (it was so hot and humid I wanted to join them), with bodies and limbs painted in various patterns, the group "played" homemade instruments, including the didgeridoo, and grunted sounds of the kookaburra bird and the dingo.

After the Aboriginal show, which was a bit shy of authentic, we watched a film that illustrated the painful story of what happened when the modern world descended upon a 40,000 year-old culture.

Later, we walked out to an open area to experience the thrill of throwing a boomerang. Most of the men got the hang of it, but the ladies had trouble sailing the boomerang outward and in most cases threw it into the ground. It was a laughable experience.

When I stepped up, a "native" showed me how to throw the boomerang; however, being left-handed didn't help. I was in league with the women who knew little about throwing anything but remarks, some encouraging. The instructor had a good laugh when the apparatus went out, turned the wrong way and never returned. It was probably made in England.

Then, it was on to Aboriginal spear chucking, using a wooden device, similar to an atlatl, in which the spear is placed to enable it to travel at a greater speed and force than possible with the unaided arm.

Additional failure fell on me. I couldn't make the device operate the way it was supposed to, so the spear I chucked traveled—with little force—about twenty feet. It was embarrassing, and the laughter from my "mates" didn't help.

I soon realized that if I had to make a living hunting animals with such a weapon, I would die of starvation quickly.

Later that evening, at the Hilton in Cairns, Sharon and I took advantage of a balcony view of the picturesque bay and whatever (costly) liquor was available in a small refrigerator. Then, it was off to dinner.

Chapter 5

Roaming Sydney

We left Cairns onboard an early morning Qantas Airlines flight heading into cloudy and drizzly Sydney. Upon arrival, we boarded a comfortable OPAL coach for a drive around the city.

Our first stop, Bondi Beach, advertised as:

AUSTRALIA'S MOST FAMOUS BEACH, A CURVING GOLDEN STRETCH OF PALE GOLD SAND AND TURQUOISE WAVES, ATTRACTING BEACH BUNNIES, SURFER DUDES AND BEACH LOVERS ALIKE.

I wasn't impressed. Maybe because it was a wet, grey day and the beach, promenade and shops were empty of day-trippers.

My trip-magnet, the "facilities," loomed out of the rain; a cold concrete bunker devoid of privacy and amenities. I was intrigued by a sign placed over the entrance:

NO CAMERAS ALLOWED IN CHANGING ROOMS

The sign obviously warned voyeurs and camera "buffs" to look elsewhere for photo ops. Since I was neither, I took my camera into the chambers without being stopped or arrested.

Next, we drove to King's Cross—also known as Sydney's red light district, and reputed to be home to organized crime groups. Once known for music halls and grand theatres, it was rapidly transformed after World War II by the influx of troops returning and visiting from the nearby Garden Island Naval Base. Today, it's a mixed locality, offering both services to nearby residents, and entertainment venues including bars, restaurants, nightclubs, brothels and strip clubs to visitors.

The bus driver said, "There are much nicer places to go out in Sydney, but if it is dodgy night clubs full of drunken teenagers then this may well be your place."

"No thanks." I said, "I get enough of that at home."

Ron added his two cents, "Be sure not to photograph bikers without asking for their permission. It is a general rule of thumb to not photograph inside tattoo parlors also."

In the future, I would avoid Kings Cross. It's no more dangerous than any other red light district in the world—not that I have frequented many of them—but it's just plain ugly. Besides, I wasn't propositioned once.

We strolled along a well-worn path, from Kings Cross to Mrs. Macquarie's Chair, high above Sydney Harbour (in deference to the Australian spelling), catching glimpses along the way of the Harbour Bridge, Opera House, and Garden Island Navy Base where the Royal Navy has docked since the early nineteenth century.

In 1810, on the peninsula named Mrs. Macquarie's Point, convicts carved out a bench from an exposed sandstone rock for the then Governor Macquarie's wife,

Elizabeth. Folklore has it that she used to sit on her "chair" enjoying the panoramic views of the harbor, and watch for ships flying the British flag, as they sailed into the port.

Mrs. Macquarie's Chair provides a bit of history as well as a beautiful view of Sydney Harbour. However, the "chair" attracts scores of tourists, and given that the seat itself is not huge, unlike some tourists' butts that so dominated the seat for photo ops, we had no opportunity to sit on it.

Nearby, the Domain stretched out for thirty-four hectares (whatever the "heck" that is) or about 8,000 acres of open space near the eastern edge of the Central Business District (CBD). It is a popular venue for outdoor concerts, open-air events, large political gatherings and rallies and is used daily by the people of Sydney for exercise and relaxation.

We paused beside a field to watch boys playing rugby. After one "scrum"—a locked-arm push from both sides into the middle over the ball—neither team could push the other out of the way to retrieve the ball. It looked like a lesson in futility, so both sides relaxed and stood up. As I raised my camera to take a picture, one lad, dressed in a garish brown and yellow combination of his team colors, posed "Hollywood" style, punctuated with two "thumbs up."

Another section of the park was laid out as a bowling green, actually tan, with "grass" like outdoor carpet, where dozens of bowlers, outfitted in all-white attire, rolled their spherical balls.

The crown jewel of the park was the Royal Botanic Gardens, which we could not peruse because of time constraints. Sharon wasn't happy since she loves all things green and colorful.

Leaving the Domain, we walked through Woolloomooloo on our way back to the bus. The current spelling of Woolloomooloo is derived from the name of the first homestead in the area, Wolloomooloo House, built by the first landowner, John Palmer.

There is debate as to how Palmer came up with the name with different Aboriginal words suggested, such as *Walla mullah*, meaning *a place of plenty*, and *Wala-mala*, meaning *an Aboriginal burial ground*. Whatever the origin, the pronunciation of the word was way more fun than the actual place.

The Woolloomooloo Wharf, also called the Finger Wharf (though which finger is anyone's guess), has some history to it. The longest timber-piled wharf in the world, it has apartments and shops that are very high end and present an antisocial atmosphere.

Back on the bus, it was a short ride to the Gap, a dip in the sandstone cliffs at the South Head peninsula facing the Tasmanian Sea.

There we walked down a footpath, but not the one I would have chosen: The 1870s cobblestone trail that leads to Lady Bay Beach, one of three in Sydney where nude bathing is lawful.

From the lookout at the top of the Gap, we looked out over a white-capped, undulating sea with giant waves crashing against the rocks below.

Although the cliff is a popular visitor destination, given the easy access, and its dramatic location at the extreme edge of the city, it has gained infamy for suicides. In 2010 one person, every two weeks jumped from these cliffs to waiting Death, and nearly one person a day comes here to think about it.

I could empathize with the thought of jumping, but not of the ennui. I stood looking over the precipice, and wondered what it would be like to fall.

Breaking up my muse, Ron said, "If you do see somebody here alone, don't be afraid to approach them. They might just want to talk or like the company. I know this from experience."

I said, "Too much time spent as a tour guide?"

He laughed, "I didn't mean personal experience."

Later that afternoon, we journeyed from the heights to the depths—the Central Business District (CBD)—popularly referred to as "town" or "the city," a suburb and main commercial center of Sydney, one of the oldest established areas in the country.

We were let loose on the streets to wander the shops and see the sights. Since Sharon and I were not in a shopping mood, we moved on to the busy heart of the city—Hyde Park, where we were welcomed by great mounds or bowls of luxurious, blooming flowers, and thousands of trees.

Strolling along a wide pathway, we observed couples lounging on the lush grass, young adults walking their dogs, and children playing games conjured up from tradition—or imagination.

Monuments dotted the landscape, including a tall statue dedicated to Captain James Cook; and the beautiful ANZAC Memorial, dedicated to remembering all Australians who have served their country; and an attraction for all convict aficionados: Hyde Park Barracks. The barracks pleasant design was the work of a reformed felon, Francis Greenway, the only convicted forger ever to be honored on a bank note.

Built in 1819 to house male convicts, the barracks later became an orphanage and later a courthouse, with each phase of its existence leaving a layer of debris that has been a gold mine for archaeologists. Today, the orange brick edifice contains a museum with a permanent collection of torture devices, including a cat-o'-nine-tails and leg irons.

Then, it was on to life on "The Rocks," a jumble of cobblestone streets and cul-de-sacs just five minutes from Circular Quay, pronounced "key." (How the Australians get that pronunciation, I will never know.)

The area was settled by convicts who, like others, colonized Australia when Britain (after the US Declaration of Independence), could no longer send misfits and criminals to the American colonies.

It was easy to stroll, shop, eat, and move from building to building, many beautifully restored from the Victorian era. Some of the shops were a wee bit crowded, but we found decent prices on all sorts of Australian "bits and pieces" such as Ugg (ugly) boots and Aussie-style hats.

This historic precinct also draws both visitors and locals with its museums and galleries, and lively weekend markets advertised as:

WHERE ELSE CAN YOU BUY DRESSES AND BAGS DESIGNED BY THE STALLHOLDER, ONE-OFF JEWELRY, ORIGINAL ARTWORKS AND PRINTS, IN A PLACE WHERE YOU CAN FEEL THE SUN ON YOUR FACE AND CATCH GLIMPSES OF OUR GORGEOUS HARBOUR.

Life was slower here and infinitely more charming, but we missed the market (poor timing), to Sharon's disappointment. She loves those places. I also missed the "sun on my face" because of intermittent rain.

We skirted most of the touristy shops; however, all that walking created a personal thirst. It wasn't long before I began to look for satiation.

I had my choice of some of the oldest pubs in Australia, such as the Hero of Waterloo, Fortunes of War, and the Lord Nelson Brewery Hotel.

I chose the Lord Nelson. Advertised as the oldest continuously licensed pub in the city, it also offered a chance to taste all six Lord Nelson micro-brews as listed in a review:

The summery beginners' Quayle ale, the bright 3 Sheets, the British-inflected Trafalgar pale ale, the full-flavoured, spicy Victory Ale, Nelson's Blood for the Guinness/porter fans, and the complex, full o' flavour Old Admiral.

Because I don't like ale, I was reluctant to drink *Nelson's Blood*, or to acquire the taste of an *Old Admiral*, so I skipped the tasting, and ordered a lager. Sharon, who doesn't care much for beer of any kind, ordered a *Nelson Nudie* cocktail made from fresh bottled juices, sans liquor.

While the lunch menu was extensive, including beef pie, which comes perched atop a mashed-potato raft in a sea of gravy, and sporting a tam-o'-shanter of mushy peas, we had our hearts set on ploughman boards of pickles, cheese, relish, mustard and pickled eggs. Gastronomically satisfied, we made our way to the Hotel Langdon, our residence for our stay in Sydney.

We were ushered into a beautiful suite overlooking Sydney Harbour, with all of the amenities such as a king sized bed, bathrobes, slippers, and the usual toilet flushing system: two push buttons, one for a full flush (fast) and one for a half flush (halfast). I even found a bathroom scale, but it measured in stones and kilos, so I just guessed at my weight, and deducted ten stones, for good measure.

In the room, I made one last attempt to reset the time and date on my wristwatch. Because we had passed through so many time zones, and because I had moved the watch's mechanism forward and backward so many times, I couldn't accomplish the task. I gave up, and took to asking others for the time, and checking out newspapers for the date.

At 4:30 p.m., we boarded a boat large enough to carry close to a hundred passengers to cruise Sydney Harbour. To help make life aboard more enjoyable, the management offered complementary wine, beer, soft drinks, and snacks, including chips and "bits and pieces" (peanuts), and Brian, our narrator.

As we passed by a mountainous residential area, I asked Ron, "What are those tracks between dwellings used for?"

He said, "They're for small inclinators, like outdoor elevators, to carry residents up and down the hills too steep to climb to reach their cars parked at either the bottom or top of the incline."

The cruise of Sydney Harbour was somewhat boring. It looked like every other harbor in the world except for the Opera House, the Harbour Bridge, and Fort Denison Island.

Brian's intermittent loud-speaker narration covering what was "out there," was interesting but it never interfered with the louder personal conversations of scores of passengers:

> Fort Denison, once known as Pinch Gut, because those who committed minor offenses could be deposited there in chains and on pitiful rations…a convict named Francis Morgan was hanged there… his remains were left to rot on the scaffold…. There are actually a dozen small islands in the harbor, all with convict connections…once the most dreaded Cockatoo Island surrounded by shark-infested waters…prisoners were squeezed into the airless barracks every night, often three to a bunk….

As we floated along, enjoying snacks and liquid lubrication, Brian's voice continued to fragment over the din:

Goat Island, where in 1835 a convict named Boney Anderson…already received some 1,200 lashes…chained naked to a rock for two years… amusement for rougher settlers…threw scraps of meat to the prisoner…Garden Island planted…to serve as a kitchen-garden by officers and crew of the First Fleet vessel, *HMS Sirus*…

As Brian finished his historical tidbits, we indulged in the "highlight" of the voyage—singing happy birthday to a perfect stranger. Most warblers were off key, which made it even more exciting.

We disembarked at Circular Quay, a popular neighborhood for both locals and tourists, consisting of walkways, pedestrian malls, parks, and restaurants. It also serves as a transport exchange for rail, bus, and ferries. Right on the harbor, it hosts restaurants, coffee shops, and weekend entertainment by street artists.

Despite its name, the waterfront at the quay is roughly square in shape. The whole area was a slice of Sydney life and very well marked for all the various rides available on the boats and ferries. I would have preferred a few more toilet facilities, especially inside the waiting area. I've learned from my travels, you can never have too many comfort stations.

Later, we gathered for dinner at the Waterfront Restaurant, on the waterfront, of course. Even though the name lacked originality, the setting was one of a kind—a distinctive replica of a square-rigged colonial sailing ship embellishes the outside dining area.

Three "masts" complete with sails and authentic rigging create the appearance of sailing aboard a clipper ship. Under the sails, umbrella-like canvas encircles the masts, some outstretched to catch the sunshine rather than the wind, and others furled to allow for creeping shadows. Mid-sails and topsails complete the arraignment. A crow's nest crowns the middle mast.

I kept waiting for the call, *"Fill the sails! Man the 'jib.'"*

Within its three-levels, Waterfront presents a range of private rooms furnished with nautical decor for both small and large groups.

A team of dedicated chefs serve a range of fresh Australian cuisine; including "flatheads," which I assumed were halibut or sole—but all I could think about was a Montana first nation's tribe.

Although the restaurant's four-course menu was decipherable, I skipped the entrée, especially the salt and pepper squid with vermicelli noodle salad and chili syrup. From the main course, I ordered a steak fillet, and from the dessert menu, the chocolate truffle cake.

The tasty steak was cooked to my specifications—"butterflied" and well done, and the cake was delicious. I returned to the hotel fully satiated.

The next day, the group, except for Sharon (too many steps), took advantage of a guided tour of the Opera House, shaped like the filled sails of a schooner, or less romantically, like egg shell quarter sections that curve over large, cathedral-like windows tinted to deflect sunlight. At a distance, the "sails" manifest a solid white exterior, but up close, thousands of small, ceramic tile squares defeat that look.

As we approached what looked like a thousand stairs ascending to the entrance, I thought that Sharon had it right by declining to join us. However, those of us who looked like we might have difficulty (in my case, a complete loss of breath) were allowed to enter the Opera House through the cavernous behind-the-scenes area underneath the facility.

After an elevator ride up several flights, we entered the first of six different performing arts venues and were guided to the best seats in the house, while our more dexterous travel-mates sat in the balcony. For once in my life, being older and less agile…helped.

The docent said, "This theater is used exclusively for opera performances, and is just one of five auditoriums. This improbable design also accommodates restaurants, bars, cafes, and shops."

Next, we visited two other theaters. In one, the biggest pipe organ I have ever seen, lofted its larger tubes at least a hundred feet upward from floor to the vaulted ceiling.

The guide said, "This is the world's largest pipe organ. It displays six divisions, five manuals plus pedals, with 131 speaking stops served by 200 ranks of 10,154 pipes."

I would have liked hearing the organ, but the organist was nowhere to be found, and phoning him was out of the question. I was sure he wouldn't pick up due to total deafness.

Our last stop inside the "sails" was at a theater in the round. It was much like the one that I used to attend in Cerritos, California, but was more attractive with beautiful birch wood paneling.

When I left the Opera complex, I looked upward at the Sydney Harbour Bridge, its steel plates and girders anchored by massive stone blocks, looking every bit like its nickname—the "Coat Hanger."

My gaze tracked the expanse of one of the longest and tallest arch-spanning bridges in the world. Even large boats plied the harbor with plenty of room to spare.

Traffic was light on the four vehicle lanes, on the two lanes used for railway tracks, and on the dedicated path for bicycles. Few pedestrians challenged a designated footpath. In fact, there were more people on top of the bridge than inside it.

I thought for a brief moment of joining a group of potential climbers ready to ascend the bridge, but perished the thought when I asked a guy in the group about the details.

He said, "It costs about $200 to climb it. Almost anyone can manage it because you are hooked together and to the bridge by harness to a safety wire all of the time. You get a protective zip-up suit and skip hat and a free group photo at the top with the bay and opera house behind. They take other photos, which you can buy if you wish. For safety, you can't take cameras or phones, or anything that might fall on the traffic below. The guides will take your personal picture at the top for a fee. On a good day the view is spectacular."

I said, "Thanks, but no thanks. It's too expensive, besides I can get the same view from my hotel room."

Ah, youth—he looked at me like I was nuts to pass up the climbing opportunity, no matter the risk or the cost.

Instead, I opted to walk across the bridge, wave at the brave souls above, and photograph views of the busy harbor—all free of charge.

Later, we drove across the "Coat Hanger" to visit the Taronga Zoo. Four volunteer docents met us and divided us into small groups. Our guide chose the Australian section to visit first, and as it turned out, last for me. The zoo was just too damned big.

Australia monopolizes the strange animal world, especially the egg laying mammals such as the platypus that, like some pubescent youngster doesn't know what he wants to be. The weird animal (not the teenager), is a fur covered, semi aquatic animal with a duck-like bill, the tail of a beaver and feet that are both clawed and webbed.

After I left the platypus swimming in a small darkened enclosure, I moved on to observe another strange animal, an echidna, similar to a hedgehog but its mouth forms a beak, and its skin ripples with long spikes.

I asked a woman next to me, "On which end is his head?"

She said, "His head is on the end away from the pointed end of the spikes."

That made sense to her, but I was still confused, "How can you tell?"

"Follow the slant of the spikes. His head is opposite the slant."

"Thanks."

I looked again, but it was still impossible to tell, so I waited for the echidna to move. When he did, I knew where his head was, unless he was walking backward.

After the mental gymnastics, I moved on to look at dingos, wombats, kangaroos, and koalas. One of the legendary reddish-brown colored wild dogs, looking every bit like a coyote with a haircut, seemed tame enough, but I knew what danger lurked behind those large black eyes. However, we were all safe since he wasn't in a howling mood, and looked like he was well fed.

Secreting themselves underground, the pig-like wombats failed to show up. I stood looking at two large holes in the earth until I felt stupid. Then, I moved on to the kangaroo range.

The kangaroos were a bit more active. They hopped about or stood around grazing in small groups. In the foreground an attendant held a baby "roo" in her lap. He was lying on his back with his dangerous feet facing her stomach—not a good position, should the little joey decide to kick.

Then it was on to the sleeping Koalas, not Koala bears. No matter that they look like cuddly teddies, they are not bears. Instead, they are marsupials.

Several sat in the crotches of fake eucalyptus trees designed for climbing to dine on real eucalyptus branches and leaves, but not while I observed them. They sat nonchalantly with eyes half closed, as if they could not care less.

In actuality, despite the myth that Koalas sleep a lot because they "get drunk" on gum leaves, most of their time is spent snoozing because it requires a lot of energy to digest their fibrous, low-nutrition diet and sleeping is the best way to conserve energy.

After I observed all that was of interest to me, I decided to walk down to the ferry port to catch a ride back to Sydney proper. Big mistake. Starting at the gift shop (where else could I find a shot glass?), I walked down one flight of stairs, and then I traversed about a hundred switchback pathways to reach the dock. Even though the two-mile trek was downhill, I was exhausted as I boarded the ferry.

By the way, ferries go everywhere around the harbor, and sail on an appreciable time table. So no matter where you are, harbor-wise, it's easy to tell if you are coming or going and you don't have to wait long to do either. If you miss one, you don't have to wait too long to catch another. It's the best way to travel to the various suburbs of Sydney.

That afternoon, in the hotel cocktail lounge we met with David Ellis, who, along with his wife, PattyAnn, had befriended Sharon and me on a previous trip. David invited us to spend some time at his lovely home, and he drove us there forthwith.

After a wonderful meal (all of the ingredients were tasty and identifiable) served by PattyAnn, and an evening of reminiscing, we reluctantly ferried back to the hotel.

The next day David and PattyAnn picked us up and drove us to Olympic Park. There, several huge towers, thirty to forty feet high, like copies of the robot, Iron Mike, lined the main boulevard, offering testament to former Olympic sites, including Los Angeles, Munich, and Melbourne.

After David parked the car, we disembarked for a walk through the Avenue of Volunteers. Scores of colorfully decorated and painted metal poles represent those who served during the Sydney Olympics. Imbedded in some of the monuments, videos played constantly, and in others, musical themes emanated without end. Both David and PattyAnn had spent hours in volunteer service to the Olympic Committee, and were rewarded with a monument of their own.

Interspersed amongst the "volunteers," were memorials dedicated to famous Australian athletes such as Cathy Freeman, living proof that some Aboriginals are good-looking.

A figure of a sprinter graces one entrance; constructed of metal sections like some huge erector set montage. The simulated sprint is so effective the metal sections appear to flake off.

Later we visited Featherdale Wildlife Park. It houses the world's largest collection of native Australian animals, and cares for over 2,200 animals, birds, and reptiles, including a twenty-foot crocodile. Well...he looked that long.

The park was a much better experience than the Torongo Zoo because it is Sydney's *ultimate* interactive wildlife experience.

Sharon cuddled a Koala named Fred, and was careful not to excite the animal (no chance) into a climbing posture—sharp claws can draw blood.

Wallabies looking like mini kangaroos with smaller legs and feet, sauntered up to the fence that bordered their enclosure. Some showed little interest in Sharon's charms or mine, but others came over for a belly scratch.

We got as close as we dared to echidnas, wombats, and Tasmanian Devils, none of which are friendly or huggable.

Two wombats sporting Doberman-like ears, and a pig-like body and face, sans snout, wandered about in their enclosure.

A Tasmanian Devil, all black with pink inner ears, and fierce looking, unhappy eyes looked like a small, short-haired dog. His red ears are the source of his moniker, not an affiliation with the crazed icon illustrated in a popular cartoon…though he did turn 360's non-stop inside the enclosure, not even pausing long enough for a decent photo.

An alligator sat by a small pond with his mouth wide open as if to say "feed me," or that he just heard a good joke. Actually, according to the keeper it's just a way of dealing with the heat by cooling out with a wide grin.

We hand-fed insatiable kangaroos that scratched our arms and hands with sharp fingernails in need of a manicure.

A sign posted next to the kangaroo enclosure caught my eye:

KANGAROO SPEAKS HIS MIND

"You think I would be happy if I had my liberty—
Don't you believe it brother, this is the life for me.
No traps, no baits, no floods or fire—
No men with guns who never tire.
Here we can eat at leisure, with friends & not with fear
Of having soup made out of our tails, for any stockman near
I like to keep my hide intact, not made into a boot—
Or maybe just a wallet for men who love to shoot.
Here we find freedom, fun & pleasure under sky of blue—
We are a happy family living at the zoo.
They love us all, they know us well, everyone by name—
Brother I feel full of Hops—
And I am very pleased I came!"

Then, it was back to the "key" for dinner at Doyle's on the Beach, Australia's first seafood restaurant. With both indoor and outdoor dining, it's located right on the foreshore of Watsons (no apostrophe) Bay overlooking Sydney Harbour.

Once again, I skipped the entrees, especially the mussels, the calamari rings fried in beer batter served with sweet chili plum sauce, and the Oysters Mornay topped with rich Béchamel Sauce. This time, I went for the flatheads with chips but without the fish sauce (chili, ginger, garlic, and coriander, whatever that is).

After dinner, I skipped the ordeal of ordering coffee: As noted before, in Australia, you have to specify a length (long or short), a color (black or white), and even an angle or level of orientation to the perpendicular (flat or not). All of it steamed. Geeze…I just wanted a *simple* cup of coffee out of a pot, not a short black, long black, or even long short black, or long or short flat white. So, I just drank my water.

Finally, it was back to the room to repack for the flight to Auckland, New Zealand. During a pause, I looked out of the window into a glowing city under a darkening storm threatening sky.

Standing there, I reminisced over my Sydney experiences. I had trouble understanding Australian English, and couldn't figure out how it had developed so differently from my own.

In addition, Sharon's former surname, "Darling," is a big hit all over Australia, especially in Sydney. Harbors, rivers, hotels, spas, politicians, sports and entertainment figures, scientists, and writers all carry the name, which made Sharon wonder if any of them were related to her former husband's ancestors. Also, it may be why she has never discouraged her hyphenated last name: "Darling-Williams."

Finally, while there is more to see in Sydney besides the Opera House and Harbour Bridge, they both seem to dominate. You can see them from every corner of the city, and if you are not careful they will magically appear in all of your photos.

The following morning, we boarded the coach and headed for the Sydney airport to leave Australia for New Zealand.

Chapter 6

Cultured Canberra

Years ago, I had previously visited Canberra, the capital of Australia, and Brisbane, one of that nation's oldest cities. Canberra was selected for the location of the nation's capital in 1908 as a compromise between rivals Sydney and Melbourne. It is unusual among Australian cities, being an entirely planned city outside of any state, similar to Washington, D.C.

The word "Canberra" is popularly claimed to mean "meeting place," from the Aboriginal designation. An alternative definition has been claimed by numerous local commentators, who have a more "vivid" imagination, whereby "Canberra" means "woman's breasts," the indigenous name for the two mountains, Black Mountain and Mount Ainslie, which lie almost opposite each other.

The same breast fetish holds true for the Grand Teton, the highest mountain in Grand Teton National Park in Wyoming. The most common explanation is that "Grand Teton" means "large teat" in French.

Our first venture in Canberra was a bus ride up one of the "breasts" (Mount Ainslie). From the tourist outlook at the summit, I enjoyed a view of central Canberra and

Red Hill to the south, the Black Mountain to the west, and the infinite grasslands that stretched out to join the Yass Plains on the north.

After filling my eyes with the panoramic present, I descended into the historic past—the Australian War Memorial that commemorates the brave soldiers who fought and died in various conflicts and also provides a living and interesting history of the nation's engagement in wars, from the colonial period to the present day.

I was most impressed with the well preserved military equipment, especially the full sized tanks outside and the airplanes inside, and the contrast of the illustrated fury of the displays with the calmness of the place.

Our bus driver/guide said, "Visiting the memorial just after Remembrance Day in November is very touching. The poppies make the walls a sea of red and it is interesting looking at the wreaths left by the various individuals and embassies."

We missed that event but I visualized the colorful tribute. Breaking up my reverie, the driver/guide said, "It's time to move on to the Parliament House."

I reluctantly joined the exiting group, feeling disappointed because we didn't get to see half of the museum.

At the Parliament House, we were supposed to see democracy in action, but Parliament was not in session. Oh well, I get enough of that at home with our stultified Congress—that when it *is* in session is not in "session."

Unlike the US Congress, where members show up when they feel like it, in capital Canberra, parliament meetings are compulsory. Time restrictions apply for both attendance and speaking, with no filibusters allowed.

We gathered in the foyer, where I perused craftsmanship tapestries, admired huge oil paintings of historical events and dignitaries (known only to the Australians), and marveled at lofty marble pillars like some gigantic stone forest that surrounded us.

We took advantage of a free guided tour of the two Houses of Parliament, similar to the British House of Commons, exhibitions and public galleries full of art, including numerous paintings of former prime ministers, and the highlight—Aboriginal letters and documents.

Back at the hotel, I caught a lift (elevator) to the bar on the grass covered roof for a view of the city, including Old Parliament, the beautiful War Memorial, and the "woman's breasts" (aforesaid mountains).

I asked the bartender, "What's the meaning of a grass growing roof?'

He said, "To illustrate the concept that the government is not above the people."

"Nice, but you could take it to mean the government is on the wrong side of the grass."

"What?"

"Under the grass."

I descended and joined the group for a bus ride to the National Art Gallery, where we were so limited in time there was no way to see it all.

I avoided any area that smacked of modern or abstract art. The meaning of art may be in the eye of the beholder, but I can't make sense of distorted or surreal images, structures made out of rocks, sticks, fake body parts, or any work that looks like it was painted by some kid in kindergarten.

I spent most of my time viewing an impressive indigenous installation featuring special exhibits of Aboriginal art that can be viewed at different levels and experienced from within.

I concluded my visit at the gift store. As usual, it seemed to be the only way out.

We left Canberra, which like many large cities in Australia is surrounded by large expanses of open country. In the distance, large flocks of sheep gathered behind what turned out to be an electrified fence.

I asked the bus driver, "Doesn't that hurt the sheep."

He said, "Only once. They are quick learners and avoid touching the fence after the first high voltage jolt that can range up to 10,000 volts."

"I'm surprised they aren't killed."

"To prevent that, not all strands are electrified, only those attached to the fence posts with black insulators, and a power energizer converts power into a brief high voltage pulse. A person or animal touching both the wire and the earth during a pulse will briefly feel a shock. It can range from uncomfortable to painful, or in few cases, death.

The situation reminded me of an old joke:

> One guy asks another, "Are all mushrooms edible?"
> The other guy answers, "Yes, but some only once."

As we drove by, I looked for charred corpses and scorched wool, but didn't see any of those detriments to living near hot wires.

It wasn't long before we arrived at a nearby sheep station established in 1880, now run by two brothers.

Emerging from the bus, I ambled toward a wooden-posted, barbed-wire fence that separated acreage. A large chain link gate stood open; the only break in the barrier that stretched to the horizon.

On the other side of the fence, the short-grass covered plain dotted with a few trees, captured my attention. A long way off, a rider on horseback, three small dots (sheepdogs, as it turned out), and a small flock of sheep appeared.

The rider approached, leaving the dogs and sheep behind. Then the Border Collies went to work. It wasn't long before they rounded up the "fur balls," and presented them in front of my fellow travelers and me.

Then, the rider, one of the brothers, the sheep, and the dogs moved through the gate opening and headed toward a small shed, where we gathered for a photo op, standing amongst the sheep.

Whenever a female traveler posed with the brothers, one of them would pinch her butt to evoke a smile. It worked—most of the time.

Eventually, one brother and the sheep disappeared inside while the dogs relaxed nearby. The other brother invited us to join him in the shed to witness the shearing process.

Inside, the shearer held the "shearee" upside down between his legs. With one hand gently holding the throat of the animal to keep it passive, the other hand moved the electric clippers over the sheep's belly, hindquarters, and neck, separating the wool from the body. He gently turned the sheep one way and then the other, always keeping one hand on the animal's throat. When the fleece had been separated in one piece, it was placed on a table, and the animal was allowed to stand in all of its nakedness—stark white in contrast to its dirty "overcoat."

Later, we enjoyed a steak dinner in a large dining room, decorated in ranch-modern with mismatched chairs and dinnerware. Hanging at one end of the room, a placard proclaimed a bit of loyalty: an Australian coat of arms including images of kangaroos and emus, two animals that can only move forward.

As we boarded the bus, one of the rascals said, "Come back again and we will throw another kangaroo on the barbie."

The drive to the airport was short as well as the flight to Brisbane, some 750 miles, comparable to the flight from Los Angeles to San Francisco.

Chapter 7

Amenities, Antiquities, and Animals

We were a small group, as I recall the bravest twelve individuals in captivity. We had previously flown to Tahiti, Fiji, and Australia in the tiniest planes, and we were transported in a small bus that was convenient—but without "convenience," and pit stops were essential. Also, the seats were designed to accommodate sixth graders or dwarfs. I couldn't find enough room for my long legs unless I chose to sit over either wheel well, which was out of the question ever since puberty.

Craig, our driver, was also our guide, or it may have been the other way around. He was responsible for narration both on the move and when we visited sites.

In Brisbane, we were escorted to the Four Points by Sheraton Hotel. "What does Four Points mean," I asked Craig.

"I think it means four stars," he said.

We piled out of the bus, and were met with a rather intimidating doorman dressed in a cutaway tux with tails and sporting a Victorian top hat. I was going to ask him what Four Points meant, but he wasn't happy seeing us wearing tourist chic, and showed some reluctance to open the door for us, so I was satisfied with Craig's explanation.

While our attire was not up to par for the doorman, it was also not appreciated in one section of the lobby, where a sign posted on a pedestal proclaimed:

ELEGANT ATTIRE IS ESSENTIAL IN THE LOUNGE

Since I didn't bring any "elegant attire" with me, I skirted the lounge and found a less arrogant place to sit while waiting for my room key.

The room on the twenty-first floor was modern and clean, and not overly pretentious, and flat-screen TV options were great. The room featured an iPod docking station, of which I had no use, since I was not into the technology craze.

I loved the double sinks in the bathroom, the large shower stall and the huge bed, but the pillows were so hard I had trouble sleeping and woke up with a sore neck. I had to walk around for a while with my head tilted to one side looking like Marty Feldman (without the pop eyes), from the movie, *Young Frankenstein*.

Later, I looked in on the budget type restaurant set up for the traveler. Austerity ruled with modern tables and chairs that looked like they had been retrieved from the '50s, all lined up cafeteria style. I chose to lunch later after exploring a bit.

Situated in the Central Business District (CBD) that stood on the original European settlement at a bend of the snaking Brisbane River, the hotel was a short walk of a few blocks to the heart of the municipality where South Bank's cultural institutions and restaurants met riverside gardens and a lagoon.

It wasn't easy to avoid the Queen Street Mall but I wasn't interested in shopping. Against the grain, I know, but I just needed a *walkabout*.

I satisfied almost every type of culture craving beneath the architecturally designed roof of the Queensland Cultural Centre on South Bank. I started in the Gallery of Modern Art, which housed more than 10,000 Australian and international artworks and was the largest of its kind in Australia. Of particular interest to me were the retrospectives on Andy Warhol. I didn't see his famous print, *Campbell's Soup Can*, but his *S & H Green Stamps* brought back memories of the days when I collected them. In any case, I couldn't understand why replicating exact images of real things was considered art.

With pictures of Warhol's "art" and scores of other odd constructions and paintings swimming around in my brain, I continued my sojourn amidst shops, restaurants, and theatres to end up at the Brisbane Arcade, which exhibits two frontages, one on the Queen Street Mall.

Exposed steel trusses shape the roof, three stories above the entrances. Natural light penetrates through clerestory windows that rise above the rooftop on each side of the central void running the length of the arcade. At the highest level, a central walkway leads to art galleries established on both sides of the cavity.

Stairs at each end access the upper levels and the Room with Roses. Advertised as one of most individual dining experiences in Brisbane, it specializes in High Tea.

Early twentieth century furnishings create the restaurant's ambiance. Chandeliers reflect light from scores of glass beads and bobbles; straight, high back chairs invite diners at most tables; at others, a small settee with pillows afford better relief; and plain china adorns all of the tables.

The name of the restaurant arose from a vase of fresh roses on the tables, the only distinction of the theme.

I looked over the menu, but couldn't find any item on it that appealed to my "naked" taste, and practical nature. Twenty-seven light meals (but not according to my wallet) were listed, including *avocado salad with cashew nuts, a light mango dressing* and *corncakes with fresh corn, capsicum, shallots, sour cream and side salad.*

More "substantial" meals (even more beyond my pay grade) included *Sweet Chicken Curry, Chicken Curry,* or *Chicken Curry served with coconut, bananas, cashews and steamed rice and pappadums.*

What you're paying for is the location and its old-world charm. If you're after reasonable value for money and a delicious sandwich, this probably isn't the place to go.

When I returned to the hotel, I dined in the unadorned restaurant. It was a whole lot cheaper, and less ambient than the Room with Roses, but when I'm hungry, I never need or wish to pay for atmosphere.

Later, I made the acquaintance of this hotel's roof top bar. To make things simple, I asked the waiter for a beer menu. The selection was extensive, including *Brisbane Bitter* (I imagined a strong taste); *Mountain Goat* (I worried about the smell); *Castlemaine XXXX* (a pornographic brew?); and *Pure Blonde* and *Skinny Blonde* (see *Castlemaine XXXX*). I finally settled for the safety of *Foster's Lager*.

The spectacular views of the CBD and the Brisbane River along with the "suds," led me into a reverie of other times and places—a nice end to the day.

The next morning, Craig guided us and related the history of the American Amphibious Base.

"In World War Two, the point was a training base for Australian and American troops and also a command post for some naval operations," he said. "In the eight months from August 1942 to March 1943, approximately twenty-five thousand Australian and American troops passed through here."

"As far as physical history goes, there is very little left on the site. However, there may still be the wells where the army derived their water supply, along with a couple of structures that might be the remains of mock ship sides, which were built so the soldiers could learn how to ascend and descend scrambling nets from ships."

The last point reminded me of the time I had to climb "up" a rope net we called a *Jacob's Ladder* strung out over the side of an LST (Landing Ship, Tank).

During a US Marine Corps landing, our amphibious tractor threw a tread, and we could only move in a circle, so we had to be towed back to the mother ship. There was no way to get off the disabled craft, except to climb some fifteen feet of netting. It wasn't easy. The first step was the most perilous. Carrying a sixty-pound pack on my back, and a forty-pound radio on my chest, I grabbed the net, placed one foot into one of rope's openings. As the small boat dropped from the crest of a wave, the bottom fell out leaving my other leg and foot dangling in thin air. I hung there without the ability to move or regain traction until two marines helped me gain a secure footing. Then, all I had to do was "drag my ass" upward to conclude my ascent.

My reverie was interrupted by Craig's request, "Please return to the bus."

From there, it was a short trip to the Lone Pine Koala Sanctuary, where we again depended on Craig's expertise. "If you make a donation, you can hold a koala."

I thought that was a good idea, so I stepped up to an attendant, offered my contribution, and received a koala to embrace. The animal hugged me, not out of affection, but just to rest its tailless body and large head. To the koala, I was just another tree crotch.

Later, we strolled around the sanctuary to visit the usual suspects, including the wombat, dingo, and Tasmanian devil. We stood for the longest time in front of an enclosure that held several "laughing kookaburras," stout, stocky birds with large heads, prominent brown eyes, and very large bills.

Craig said, "The name, laughing kookaburra, refers to the bird's laugh, which it uses to establish territory amongst family groups. One bird starts with a low, hiccupping chuckle, and then throws its head back in raucous laughter. Often several others join in."

I said, "Are they bashful in front of people? I haven't heard a peep from any of them."

"It's probably the time of day. They laugh most frequently shortly after dawn and after sunset to dusk."

"Maybe it's that dog barking that keeps them silent."

"That's probably not a dog, but rather a barking owl."

"Can we go look at it."

"We can try, but most people hear the barking owl rather than see it."

As we got closer, the vocalization was in the form of a double "hoot," like a double dog bark that so closely resembles a small dog that it was difficult to tell the difference.

Craig said, "Barking calls can be varied in pitch and intensity, including growls, howls, screams, bleating and twittering, depending on the purpose of the call."

As we got closer, the owl went mute, and as Craig had indicated, it also became invisible, so we moved on to the kangaroo area that included a zone where they could retreat from people. However, once visitors bought corn, that space remained empty, and the charge was on.

I held out my hand full of corn to the insatiable "roos." When they felt that I wasn't giving them enough, they scratched at my hand with sharp nails. Greedy bastards!

Then, it was back to the hotel where I once again found solace in the Sheraton's roof top bar.

Chapter 8

Auckland Adventures

B ack to the future: We bid farewell to Australia, flew across the Tasmanian Sea on a private airplane owned by Tauck Tours—a two engine prop job that was so quiet, we could listen to music from the '40s and '50s over the intercom—and landed in Auckland, situated north of almost everything on the North Island of New Zealand.

Looking out the window before we touched down, I could see why Auckland is known as the "City of Sails." Not only because of its spectacular waterfront location, but more likely because one in every four adults owns a boat.

Australia and New Zealand are part of the Southern hemisphere's antipodes (pronounced, an-TIH-puh-deez). Over 600 years ago, the word appeared in a translation of a Latin text as a term designating "men that have their feet against our feet," that is, inhabitants of the opposite side of the globe, which, for some strange reason, gave rise to the early British belief that all of the "Antipodeans" walked with one large foot.

Due to an almost paranoid fear of foreign agriculture and products, all luggage is X-rayed upon arrival.

Unfortunately, a raisin showed up in my carry-on, and for a moment I thought I might be arrested for not declaring it. However, I was granted a reprieve when the "discoverer" said, "It's not too late to declare your agricultural product."

I said, "Thanks."

I admitted to the ownership of the grape that had shriveled during transit, then, I trashed it.

My attention turned to the kangaroo leather hat, purchased for Arney, my stepson, and hand carried all over Australia. Because of perceived animosity between the two countries, I wasn't sure the authorities would allow something made in Australia entry into New Zealand.

Relieved that no questions occurred about the hat, I quickly picked it up, gave it to Sharon, and gathered up our luggage.

We were in need of coffee, so we stopped at a small shop. Faced with the same choices that made no sense to us in Australia, such as *short black, long black, flat white*, sans *Americano*, we ordered a latte to go, and met our now familiar guide, Ron, who herded us through the exit to the waiting tour bus.

As we rolled along, Ron said, "With its influx of Asian and Polynesian immigrants, Auckland is the most multicultural, cosmopolitan city in New Zealand. As such, its citizens have developed a passion for panache in defiance of the *tall poppy syndrome*, the dictum that requires no one stands out from the crowd. It's enough to make a rural New Zealander fall face first into his flock of sheep."

Echoes From Down Under

I said, "We're not bothered by that condition in the states, since celebrity and wealth are revered. By the way, what's the date and time?"

Mentally, I registered Ron's answer, and then tried to apply it to my watch. I noticed that the time difference between Sydney and Auckland was two hours, and the date was a day ahead, however, because my watch was so confused from several previous time and date changes, I, again, gave up correcting it, and just figured to hell with it.

We were lodged in the five-star Langham Hotel on the fourth floor where our cultural and financial status was established: *Superior*, first through fourth floors; *Deluxe*, fifth through eighth floors; and *Executive*, ninth through tenth floors.

While we stayed in a less expensive room, the view was the same as higher up, and we, in our tourist garb, shared the same elevator as those from the upper crust floors who were more stylishly dressed.

On the ground floor, when the crowd emptied out of the lift, we were easy to spot. Ron came over and asked, "How's your room?"

I said, "The room is nice, but in looking over the hotel menu, the food is out of my price range. Are there some less expensive places to eat nearby?"

"Yes, a short walk will reward you with plenty of places at half the price to satisfy your palate and your wallet, but avoid DaVinci's across the street as it is not Italian, and the New York/Rat Pack aesthetic is dated and inappropriate."

Before we left the hotel, I went looking for a shot glass. In my search, I somehow wandered into a health and beauty shop. Hundreds of hair, skin, and vitamin products lined the shelves, including a supplement made from sheep placentas (no shortage of these in New Zealand) for "well-being," however, I was feeling sick just reading the label.

Once I found the appropriate gift shop, I purchased a shot glass, available for Auckland—but not for the hotel. Then, it was out the door to lunch up the street, at Bella's Café, which wasn't a whole lot less expensive, but at least the place was real Italian. We had a chicken wrap.

After lunch, we returned to the hotel to board our bus for a tour of Auckland, first down Queen Street and then along the waterfront.

Stretched out for what seemed like miles, the main shopping venue, Queen Street, hosts a wide variety of stores, shops, banks, and restaurants.

Ron said, "Because it is known by reputation all over the country, even by people who have never seen it, Queen Street is the prime destination for locals and visitors alike."

His words rang true: The sidewalks were crammed with all manner of human beings, and the road was jammed with busses, cars, taxis, and even jay-walking pedestrians. It was slow going, much to the delight of the ladies on board who could hold their gaze for some time on individual shopping ops.

The hustle and bustle continued even after the street culminated at the wharf and ferry stops. From there, we trundled along the waterfront.

Ron said, "Waitematā Harbor is the main access by sea to Auckland. Well sheltered, not only by the Hauraki Gulf itself but also by Rangitoto Island, the harbor offers good protection in almost all winds."

The water sparkled like the obsidian, named Waitematā, that early Māori settlers found in the area. Bright sunshine reflected off the sails of numerous small boats and a few yachts that meandered, while unwavering ferries darted to and fro over the dark water.

With its distinctive symmetrical volcano cone rising 850 feet over the Hauraki Gulf, Rangitoto delivers a menacing backdrop to the pristine scene.

A number of Māori myths exist surrounding the volcano, including that of a tupua couple. After quarreling and cursing Mahuika, the fire-goddess, they lost their home on the mainland because it was destroyed by Mataoho, god of earthquakes and eruptions, on Mahuika's behalf. Lake Pupuke on the North Shore was created in the destruction, while Rangitoto rose from the sea. The mists surrounding Rangitoto at certain times are considered the tears of the tupua couple for their former home.

It wasn't far to the Auckland War Memorial Museum, or simply the Auckland Museum. Dominating the skyline, the neo-classical styled building sits prominently on the crater rim of a dormant volcano in the Auckland Domain, a large public park.

The copper and glass dome, as well as the viewing platform—with its event center underneath—had been criticized by some as resembling a collapsed soufflé, but quickly won the admiration of critics and public, noted for its undulating lines that blend in with the volcanic landscape and hills.

Embedded in blue tile at the entrance is a depiction of a large sandy-colored fern-like wreath that reaches up to commemorate those New Zealanders killed in action, and encircles a bold-faced inscription:

LEST WE FORGET

An extensive exhibition illustrates wars, both within New Zealand and New Zealand's participation in overseas conflicts.

I was most interested in the original WWII Spitfire and Mitsubishi Zero airplanes that were in excellent shape. Reminiscing, I could hear the whine of the starters and the roar of the engines in preparation for takeoff into deadly combat. Like all of the military weapons on display, the planes were larger in reality than in the world of war films I have relished over the years.

The museum also provides a home for the world's largest collection of Māori and Polynesian artifacts and treasures, as well as three *entire* buildings, including Hotunui, a large carved meeting house.

I was especially intrigued with a "waka taua" (war canoe) from 1830, one of the world's longest war canoes (approximately fifty feet long) made out of a single oak log. I'm sure it was difficult to carve the canoe out of one of the hardest of woods, but launching that sucker must have been even more challenging, worth a double hernia at least. It probably took the whole village.

The Māori cultural show, included in our tour, delivered prodigious grunting, stomping, and threating, exceptionally long tongue wagging from the male dancers, as opposed to the females who gracefully danced, moved their hands and arms, and twirled their balls to and fro. I most appreciated the dancers who wore grass skirts and coconut shell bras. I wondered if the coconuts came in sizes, such as A, B, and C—a D cup size was out of the question as it would have been one hell of a large coconut.

After the special presentation of stimulating Māori dances and entertainment, I had to take several pictures of Sharon being hugged by a tattooed, really buffed out Māori warrior. She said it was because people kept getting in the way, but I think she just liked to be next to the guy.

Outside, encompassing all of the crater and most of the surrounding tuff ring of the Pukekawa (puke away if eruption occurs) volcano, the Domain, Auckland's oldest and largest park, swells outward to seventy-five hectares (whatever that is).

Several sports fields occupy the crater floor, circling to the south of the cone, while the rim opposite the museum hosts the cricket pavilion and Auckland City Hospital.

Higher up on the north side of the central scoria—the highly vesicular, dark colored volcanic rock—two large glass greenhouses dominate the scene.

A fernery, showcasing New Zealand native plants, rises out of an old quarry in part of the cone, and wild and woolly duck ponds thrive in the northern sector of the explosion crater, breached by a small overflow stream.

On the way back to the hotel, we were dropped off at Queen Street. It was hard work dogging crowds gathered around street performers and pedestrians bent on running into us. It seemed that everyone in the city was walking the streets (in a shopping sense).

We shunned high end and boutique stores and more restaurants and coffee shops than I could count, looking for souvenir shops where we could find objets d'art and of course, shot glasses, reminders of our journey.

Later, hosted by Tauck Tours, we dined at CinCin (pronounced Chin Chin, no pun intended), on the Quay (key) Restaurant. The best thing about CinCin is the setting—a very unique location in the old Ferry Building overlooking the water.

CinCin is a fashionable restaurant and one of the oldest established eateries in the city, serving six courses with a wine match; a bit of everything from Pacific Rim specialties, to New Zealand lamb and venison, and Italian dishes. They even do pizzas.

I thought it was a bit over rated. Ironically, the smaller the portions, the more garnish with non-edible stuff, and the higher the cost. I had the Pan Fried Snapper. It was at least recognizable.

As we walked back to the hotel from the CinCin Restaurant, scores of teenage girls, in groups of four or five, dressed in various costumes, on a scavenger hunt sponsored by the local radio station, asked people on the street and in the shops for miscellaneous items.

While watching the parade of girls, I heard Sharon laugh behind me. When I turned around, two girls had their hands and forearms down the back of Sharon's blouse. At first I thought she was being mugged, but the girls assured me, they just wanted her bra.

As Sharon contorted one way and then another, she finally said she couldn't remove it on a public street, so the girls called out for scissors to just cut a size tag from it. However, they gave up bra-diving when they found out Sharon's bra wasn't big enough—single D (they wanted a DD cup size) and finally left her alone.

I wanted to help them pursue the achievement of their goal, but Sharon would have none of it.

The next day we visited archeologist and diver Kelly Tarlton's Sea Life Aquarium, set on the waterfront of Okahu Bay. There, he built a 360 foot tunnel created from disused sewage storage tanks. Then, he developed a new method of building an acrylic lining that allowed 360-degree viewing rather than flat panel observations only.

We stepped onto a people-mover that slowly proceeded in a wide circle. I looked up as fish sashayed over my head. It was a weird feeling, almost as if I was scuba diving, yet unencumbered with tanks, mask, and rebreather.

There were a couple of problems in viewing the native marine life of the southern oceans. One, because of the refraction caused by light traveling through water, and the acrylic sheets used in the creation of the tunnel, the fish appear to be one third smaller than they really are. And two, I couldn't tell what kind of fish I was looking at since none of them were labeled. Can you tattoo fish?

However, I was having so much fun, I went around twice while Sharon who wasn't that thrilled, waited for me to return.

Then, it was off to the Antarctic Ice Adventure, the temperature controlled habitat of king penguins and gentoo penguins (those that are less aggressive). While looking through glass, I could tell the difference because of size, but they all looked alike, "dressed for dinner."

Leaving the birds garbed in their tuxedos, we passed through a recreation of the hut used by Captain Robert Falcon Scott during his South Pole expedition in 1912. It wasn't much, but it was a lot warmer than the original, I'm sure.

Another section was filled with sharks, including bronze whalers, sevengill sharks, wobbegongs, and school sharks, but no great whites for obvious reasons.

It was easy to spot the bronze whalers and the sevingills, but not the wobbegong (none of them looked depressed), nor school sharks (classes were not in session).

For a fee, visitors can join the fish (unlike a historical mobster related East River experience in New York) in a shark cage encounter or cage-less shark fearful experience, where dive professionals act as guides during these swims, and help ensure that the familiarity is safe.

I thought the safety feature was credible as far as the guides were concerned but I wondered if the sharks had been told to be nice. In any case, I wasn't wearing a bathing suit, so I had a great excuse to avoid both circumstances.

I learned from a nearby attendant that the sharks are held only for a short period of time before being released back into the sea, probably because all sharks can be trusted, some only once.

At Stingray Bay, we looked into a huge, open topped acrylic tank containing stingrays, including "Phoebe," a 550-pound, short-tail stingray with a seven-foot wingspan.

Smaller aquariums nearby provided homes for single species of sea life, including red-bellied piranha (I took their word for the belly color), an octopus, sea horses, moray eels, crayfish, stonefish, and pufferfish.

Conveniently located near the exit, the gift shop baited human "fish" to purchase mementos. I was reeled in for a shot glass that wasn't much, but had to suffice.

Before we returned to the hotel, we departed the bus at the base of the Sky Tower, a 1,076-foot tall observation and telecommunications edifice, reminiscent of Seattle's Space Needle. Measured from ground level to the top of the mast, it's the tallest freestanding structure in the Southern Hemisphere.

We avoided the casino, restaurants, and live theater at the lower levels, and rode an elevator up to the main observation level at 610 feet just below the restaurant which turns 360 degrees every hour, and the brasserie-style (no relation to the aforementioned "DD cup") buffet.

We stood looking straight down through one and a half inch thick glass sections of flooring. Sharon could hardly look through the glass without feeling ill, but I, hoping the glass would not crack and give way, looked down a little longer, feeling like James Stewart in the film, *Vertigo*.

To "enhance" any sick feelings that you might harbor, the tower features the Sky Jump, a 630-foot launch from the observation deck, reaching speeds up to fifty-three miles per hour, the jump is guide-cable-controlled to prevent jumpers from colliding with the tower in case of wind gusts, but nothing is provided to keep you from upchucking your lunch onto unsuspecting tourists below.

Still a bit dizzy from our tower experience, we walked, not exactly straight, back to the hotel and up to our room to relax and prepare for tomorrow's trip to Rotorua.

Chapter 9

Ramblin' Rotorua

From Auckland, we traveled by coach. Thankfully, it was a no-fly day, through lush farmlands into the scenic heart of the North Island. I observed cattle, deer, and upper class horses (those wearing blankets), and thousands of sheep that when they saw the bus coming, turned to show their posteriors—not their best feature.

We stopped at the Huntly Power Station to view a unique steam vented power plant, but more importantly to relieve the "traveler's curse."

The largest thermal power station in New Zealand rose up like some giant tinker-toy erection, a hum emanated from its two 250 MW coal-and-gas-fired steam turbines that supply over thirty-one percent of the country's current (not to be confused with power) electricity needs.

While in the gift shop, I got my first look at possum sweaters and jackets, not those worn by possums, but those advertised as "made from a blend of two of nature's finest fibers—hand selected possum fur and superfine merino wool."

Posted in the middle of the pile, a placard read:

EACH NIGHT THE POSSUMS IN NEW ZEALAND EAT
22,000 TONNES OF OUR FORESTS. THE COMMERCIAL
USE OF POSSUM FUR FIBRE IS THUS ENCOURAGED BY
CONSERVATION GROUPS AND PLAYS AN IMPORTANT ROLE
IN THE PROTECTION OF NEW ZEALAND'S NATIVE FAUNA,
FLORA AND WILDLIFE. YOUR PURCHASE NOT ONLY MEANS
THAT YOU HAVE ACQUIRED A UNIQUE GARMENT THAT WILL
GIVE YOU YEARS OF PLEASURE, BUT ALSO THAT YOU HAVE
CONTRIBUTED TO THE PRESERVATION OF NEW ZEALAND'S
NATURAL BEAUTY.

The possum sweaters and jackets were attractive, and I am a great believer in conservation, but I knew I would never wear either one in Southern California. Instead, I satisfied my shopper's itch by purchasing a power station shot glass to add to my collection of over 950 of the "wee drams."

Later, we stopped for lunch at Longlands Farm, a combination working farm and country garden, where I learned more than I wanted to know about dairying, calving, breeding, and even sweetbreads—not those sweetbreads! These were from the thymus glands of sheep.

The drive to the farm was lined with trees emblazoned with golden and maroon leaves that contrasted with the green, fertile valleys of the Hamilton-Waikato farming area of Matamata.

When we disembarked at the main building, we walked across a wide porch where log chairs greeted us in case we wanted to later sit and enjoy the view.

We entered a British style dining area complete with polished wooden tables decorated with roses, and curved-back wooden chairs, a fireplace, a small bar with two stools placed in front, and various beer and wine products lined up in the back. At one end of the bar, a strange looking porcelain crock dispatched tap beer from the two attached spigots. Long beams traversed an open ceiling, supported by poles at a few locations. Chandeliers, revealing bulbs shaped like candles, dangled from the heights.

The host presented us with a welcome drink and provided a description of the farm's activities and functions. Then, we were invited to a memorable lunch with barbecued leg of lamb, roasted farm vegetables, and for dessert, a dip-your-own homemade vanilla ice cream concoction. No double-dipping allowed. Everything was fresh, more like a home cooked meal from your favorite aunt than one from a restaurant.

After lunch, we enjoyed wandering over the wide expanse of lawn and into a garden full of native shrubs, flowers, and trees within a patio-like setting. Arbors partially shaded some of the plants, such as the Feijora, a fruit similar to guava but with a scent.

It was all I could do to convince Sharon to leave and return to the porch for a final panoramic view of the farm and grounds.

It's easy to see why these green pastures and rolling hills were chosen to portray Hobbiton and The Shire from the movie, *The Lord of the Rings*. Hobbit fans can visit the movie set on a guided tour that includes more than forty-four unique hobbit holes, and Bag End (Bilbo's house).

I wasn't impressed with the movie and even less so with a chance to visit the set location, after all, it was just a bunch of holes in the ground that looked like some animal, a possum perhaps, had been digging for grubs.

As we turned toward Rotorua, I observed large, clear plastic spheres like giant soap bubbles rolling down a grassy incline.

I said, "Ron, can we stop and take a look?"

He said, "Okay, but if anyone wants to ride in one of the balls, called Zorbs, it has to be quick, since we have reservations at the Agrodome, down the road."

After we departed the bus for a closer look, I asked Ron for details.

He said, "The ride costs $25 to $45 depending on the mode you choose: dry, wet, or with a body board. They've got all kinds of weird names for each type, Zorbit, Zydro, and Zurf. Once you have made your choice, you tumble approximately sixty-five yards downhill harnessed inside the sphere. Zorb is very safe, as there is a cushion of air between you and the ground. The ride lasts about ten seconds, reaching speeds of up to twenty miles per hour."

There were no takers, including me. Besides, it was rumored that the Zorbit ride produced the impression of what a sperm feels like trying to fertilize an egg, and the liquid in the Zydro and Zurf balls was the accumulated urine of everyone that pissed themselves previously hurtling down the hill.

After lunch, we visited the world famous Agrodome near Ngongothaha (a place where you can go to a have a good laugh) to learn everything about sheep farming, well—almost everything. When faced with too much information all at once, I retreat into to my usual attitude: "I don't really give a shit."

As we drove up, sheep, as if to greet us, gathered at the fences that lined the roadway, but cows couldn't have cared less, although we got a lazy look from a couple of them. They were a mixed bag (no pun intended), such as Herefords, Jerseys, Guernseys, and "Oreos"—black on both ends with a wide white stripe in the middle.

We disembarked from the bus, entered the Agrodome, a huge farm shed, and found a place to sit on one of the long wooden benches.

Rams, representing nineteen breeds of sheep, entered the stage, one by one, and found their place behind placards that described their breed. No confusion ensued, since the rams had accomplished this feat a million times before.

I looked at Sharon who was enthralled, and I said, "Their actions remind me of the old joke about New Zealand sheep."

She said, "Oh no, not the one about how to make a ewe turn."

"No, it's cleaner and more relevant."

"Okay, tell me."

"Some pundit once said 'New Zealand is a country of eighty million sheep, four million of which think they are human.'"

"Ha Ha, that's probably true."

I couldn't get over how placid the rams were, all decked out in their wool suits, including the Merino that looked like a large cotton ball with hooves.

The sheep were entertaining, but left the jokes to the master of ceremonies, who in a humorous way, conveyed information about the type of wool each animal produced, and whether or not they were good for fleece, for "dinner," or for both.

Then, a sheep dog appeared from the stage cupboard herding a group of geese. While the dog stopped in mid-stride, the geese waddled on across the stage to disappear behind a barrier. Then, the goose-herder joined three other dogs to jump upon and run *across* the backs of the lined-up sheep, stopping just long enough to pose for a photo or two, and then continue on before dropping down to the deck and exiting.

This was followed by a sheep shearing demonstration, and a simulated sheep auction.

I said, "Hon, keep your hands folded in front of you."

Sharon asked, "Why?"

"Because the auctioneer looks for the slightest finger movement from individuals in the audience to start or increase the bid on any particular animal."

We sat perfectly still, while a guy from Japan brushed a fly away from his face and won a live sheep.

I was invited up to the stage to milk a cow, which I had accomplished years ago when I stayed on a Montana farm. I must have lost my touch because no matter how hard I squeezed and pulled, no milk emanated from the teats. As I sat there frustrated, an attendant approached and told me how to do it. Following his instructions, I was able to finally make the nipples squirt.

I earned a *Certificate of Udderance* to prove I actually completed one of the trickiest little operations on a farm.

Outside, we were treated to a working demonstration of sheep herding by Huntaway (barking) sheep dogs and Strong Eye dogs that gave the sheep a look only a mother-in-law could appreciate.

Then, it was off to Rotorua, or the full name from the Māori: *Te Rotorua-nui-a Kahumatamomoe*; *roto* means lake, and *rua* means two, or second lake.

Kahumatamomoe (I no longer have hammer toe) was the recipient of the second lake dedication from an ancestral explorer.

As we drove through the outskirts of Rotorua, I noticed a cemetery strewn with stark white vaults like those found in New Orleans, holding deceased residents above geothermal activity rather than above water.

With some trepidation, we left the bus to walk through a small version of Yellowstone called the Whakarewarewa Thermal Village, now called Te Puia, which is much easier to pronounce.

Prone to geothermal activity from deep within the earth's core, sulfur dioxide seeps through cracks and craters and fills the air with an acrid stench. Amid the smoking rifts and seething pools, boiling mud bubbles, and steaming geysers shoot high into the sky. Water oozes down otherworldly, scorched white terraces. Pools and lakes take on hues of blue, green, pink, and yellow.

The last time I was in Rotorua I stayed at the Rotorua Hotel, located so close to the geothermal action, the pool was heated by thermals rising from fissures in its bottom. The hotel no longer exists. I suspect it finally blew up.

Since the town lies on a caldera, the Māori actually live and cook amongst the hot pools and steam vents, but leave the bubbling mud to the tourists.

We left the land of geysers, no telling when they would go off, much like our warrior guide, and headed to the Māori Cultural Center. Tattooed from head to toe, wearing the smallest of loincloths, he was threatening, thrusting and waving a spear, stomping from side to side, and sticking out his large tongue, but then he smiled and I knew we were not to be sacrificed to some ancient god, so we followed him. I'm sure the women in the group enjoyed the rear view. I learned later that the tongue wriggling is considered a friendly gesture like the wagging of a dog's tail.

The Māori center is plain in design with carved symbols over the entrance at the peak of the gabled roof. Tall, engraved poles, resplendent with symbolic representations of gods and life, hugged each corner of the building.

Inside, we observed wood carvers at work on masks, totems, and a small canoe. After we passed exhibits detailing Māori village life, we found ourselves at a section where women weaved clothing from flax, and fabricated dancing skirts from palm leaves, rolled into tight cylinders, some eighteen inches long, closely lined up side by side, and stitched together into a belly band in such a way that all of the dancers' "possibles," would be covered.

Māori Warrior heritage is played out in the *haka*, that frenzy of grunting, eye-rolling, chest slapping, foot stomping, and tongue protruding traditional war cry, dance, or challenge from the Māori people.

War haka (plural) were originally performed by warriors before a battle, proclaiming their strength and prowess in order to intimidate the opposition, but haka are also performed for various reasons: for welcoming distinguished guests, or to acknowledge great achievements, occasions or funerals, and *kapa* (meaning *row* or *rank*) *haka* performance groups are very common in schools.

The New Zealand sports teams' practice of performing a *haka* before their international matches has made the haka more widely known around the world.

After the energetic dances, we joined others for a geothermally cooked *Hāngi* meal, a traditional New Zealand Māori method of cooking food.

To "lay a *hāngi"* involves digging a pit in the ground, heating stones in the pit with a large fire, placing baskets of food on top of the stones, and covering everything with earth for several hours before uncovering (or lifting) the *hāngi*.

The feast delivered fresh meats and seafood, including huge prawns, and steamed oysters at the table. I especially enjoyed the unlimited coffee and the desert—cake, berries, and ice cream.

Following the exhilarating and satiating visit to the cultural center, we were off to a more sedate experience—the kiwi enclosure, which housed the bird rather than the fruit.

Inside it was so dark I had to feel my way to the magenta-lighted glass cage. Others shared the touchy-feely experience so much it created raucous laughter. I was sure the humor wasn't appreciated by the kiwi. If they had appeared they were now long gone, huddled away in frightened seclusion. In any case, I didn't see the bird, and no one I spoke to actually saw it.

As I understand it, the female kiwi, a brown bird about the same size as a bantam chicken, but with thin, spindly legs, a long foraging beak and useless stubby wings, insists on laying an egg so big (almost as large as the kiwi itself) that her tummy sometimes drags along the ground. In the final days before laying, she can't eat at all because so much of her belly is taken up by her egg, which grows to six times the magnitude of eggs of similar sized birds. Then delivery—ouch!

Next, it was off to the Duxton Hotel at Okawa Bay. As I approached, I observed the front of the hotel, where at ground level and one floor above, French doors opened onto balconies furnished with wicker chairs inviting occupants to sit and take in the view of the expanse of lawn leading down to a beautiful lake.

Inside, the management met us with a warm welcome and a complimentary drink. We stood around imbibing and chatting for a while until the room keys were passed out. Needless to say our room was not located on the scenic side of the hotel, and a balcony was of little use since it didn't exist.

However, after we settled in, we walked downstairs and out the front door to the lawn and strolled down to the lake. As we passed a couple, the man said, "Watch out for the 'oompah.'" Sharon didn't understand the warning, so I explained the term from an old joke, while pointing out the scattered presence of droppings from birds that never suffered constipation.

Chapter 10

Mountains, Myths, and Mother Nature

We said goodbye to our local guide, and waited in the Rotorua airport, a facility so small, we had to leave our luggage outside for fear of tripping over it. "We entered the same door as out we left" to later board a small non-jet, over the wing twin-engine airplane.

"Does it seem like the planes are getting smaller and smaller?" I asked Sharon.

She said, "Yes. I didn't realize we would have to fly so many times on this trip, especially in tiny planes."

"Well, these aren't nearly as small as some I flew in the last time I visited this area. Since we were a small group, we had to make our own flight reservations. At Rotorua, I called the airport, and said, 'My wife (first spouse) likes an aisle seat and I like a window seat.' The reservations clerk said, 'They are both. The plane holds six passengers, three on each side of an aisle.'

Because Tahiti and Fiji were additions to our itinerary, we flew twenty-two times on that trip. I thought I was growing feathers, and began to wonder if all of my flight chips were used up."

Presently, we flew so low over the Southern Alps I worried about crashing, but what a view: under bright sunshine and an intense blue sky, jutting mountains, massive snowfields, rocky moraines, azure lakes, and glacial valleys drifted in and out of sight.

Landing at the non-descript airport near Mount Cook, we exited the plane, collected our luggage, and entered a small building just large enough to provide a waiting area and restrooms. No staff was present which was a blessing since we didn't have to face another invasive, obnoxious security check.

At 12,218 feet, Mount Cook/Aoraki is the highest mountain in New Zealand. It lies in the Southern Alps, the mountain range which runs the length of the South Island.

Mountaineers regard the area to be the best climbing region in Australasia, including Sir Edmund Hillary who climbed there in preparation for his conquest of Everest.

Aoraki, the Māori name for Mount Cook derives from an early name for the South Island, *Te Waka o Aoraki* (Aoraki's Canoe or Cloud Piercer).

According to Māori legend, Aoraki was a young boy who, along with his three brothers, was the son of Rakinui, the Sky Father. On their voyage around the Papatuanuku, the Earth Mother, their canoe became stranded on a reef and tilted. Aoraki and his brothers climbed onto the top side of their canoe. However, the south wind froze them and turned them to stone. Their canoe became the Te

Waka o Aoraki, the South Island, and their prows, the Marlborough Sounds. Aoraki, the tallest, became the highest peak, and his brothers created the Kā Tiritiri o Te Moana, the Southern Alps.

We stayed at the Hermitage Hotel at the base of Mount Cook. Far from being a hermitage, the five star, ten story hotel is built like a chalet, with satellite cabins for backpackers and others who want to "rough it." The hotel actually backed up to dense chaparral and small bushes that climbed a rocky incline, but at first glance the structure appeared to be built into the hillside.

Because we were with a tour, I feared that we would be placed in a room facing the scrubs. However, my worries were unfounded, since all rooms in the main body face Mount Cook.

For some strange reason, we rode an elevator up two levels, then walked a long hallway to enter another elevator to access the resident floors—five through ten.

We left the elevator at the sixth floor, and found our room. To establish the likelihood of good fortune, I quickly opened the drapes covering a large window: At ground level the pool, dressed in chaise lounges and umbrellas, and peeked-roofed auxiliary buildings bothered the flatness of the immediate landscape. In the distance snow covered mountains that looked like the Colorado Rockies, jutted upward into a cloudless sky.

Later, we enjoyed the same view from bar stools in the lounge.

I said, "Hon, I think I'll order a Cadillac margarita."

Sharon said, "I don't think that's such a good idea since it just confuses bartenders outside of the United States. Just keep it simple."

"Okay, but simple always turns into complex, especially when it comes to the mix."

Not wanting to go through the "Yes, we have no 7-Up or Sprite," ordeal, I ordered a beer. Sharon passed on her usual martini, and ordered a vodka tonic.

We enjoyed the pricey dinner buffet on Tauck Tours, and retired to our room. I turned out the lights, and looked out at a jet black sky stuffed with stars. The Milky Way and constellations were visible even though the moon was nearly full.

Getting ready for bed, I entered the bathroom and was introduced to a flat-slab wash basin. I gingerly turned on the hot water, waiting for it to splash onto my crotch (the usual destination for wild water), but by some miracle it didn't leap at me. Oh, the marvels of plumbing.

Later the next day, we stepped outside to enjoy nature and walk to the base of Mount Cook. Having no desire to climb the mountain, I stood for a long moment at a point where several trails beckoned as in Robert Frosts' poem, "The Road Not Taken." The paths were tempting but it was getting close to five o'clock somewhere, so I, along with Sharon, returned to the hotel bar.

That evening, we were invited to avoid the buffet and join the group for a sit-down, from-a-menu dinner. I enjoyed the tomato-bacon soup. Anything with bacon in it pleases my taste buds, but I didn't eat the entrée—I couldn't figure out what it was. The fillet mignon was very good, except it was placed on what was supposedly a rice cake, but I am sure it was Styrofoam; I didn't take a bite to find out.

After too short a stay at the Hermitage, comprised of wandering around in an awestruck state and snapping far too many photos of scenery, we once again returned to the desolate airport.

It was a bright morning full of promise and at the same time regrets as the sun once again highlighted Mount Cook.

We took off in our private prop-job, and flew south toward Te Anau at a low altitude, just above the sheep backs (clouds), which separated at times to provide brief views of alpine lakes, herb fields, and white capped mountains, including Mount Aspiring, so named, I suspect, because it endeavors to reach the height of Mount Cook.

Chapter 11

Te Anau Treasures

Just before we touched down the pilot said the runway was too short so we would have to land partially on the grass in front of it. I wasn't crazy about the idea, since the grassy areas I could see out of the window were flooded from a recent rain. I worried that the landing gear would be left behind in the soft earth and we would have to make a "belly landing." However, we made it with wheels intact and a few inches of runway to spare.

We disembarked the plane, boarded a waiting bus, and departed for the Te Anau Hotel and Villas conveniently located directly across the road from Lake Te Anau, and around the corner from the main road into town.

Ron booked us into the hotel, passed out room keys, and distributed and explained an activity itinerary. What he failed to describe was the lack of an elevator.

Since our room was on the second floor, I searched for the lift but failed to find it. I returned to the desk and asked a clerk, "Where have you hidden the elevator?"

He said, in the true sense of 'yes, we have no elevators,' "The hotel doesn't have any, but the stairs are not steep and long."

So saith the one who didn't have to carry the luggage up the steps.

With a great deal of effort we dragged two suitcases and two carry-ons up, one step at a time, to reach the second floor landing. Then, it was a pushover (pun intended) to the room.

The small, dated accommodation was clean, comfortable, and afforded an excellent view of the placid, deep waters of Lake Te Anau and its western shore bordered by a dense, green forest.

That evening, we joined our travel-mates for the customary get-to-know-you reception and dinner. After a few glasses of wine, funny looking "whore's drawers" (hors d'oeuvres), and a lot of conversation, I was ready to sit down for the four course meal: Starter, soup or salad, entree, and dessert. Skipping the starter, I ordered the soup and the salmon. The soup was delivered promptly, which was a nice touch that saved me from staring into space while others finished their first course.

By the time I received the salmon, the course order arrangement had smoothed out. However, I was presented with a new challenge—what to do with the sauces and dabs of stuff on top of the fish.

After scraping and pushing the trappings to one side of the plate to reveal, in all of its nakedness, the salmon, I dug in.

The following morning we were off to Te Anau and Milford Sound. As we approached Te Anau, Ron said, "The picturesque township of Te Anau encourages outdoor activities, shopping, and dining. It also has a cool movie theatre that shows a local production of the movie, *Fiordland National Park*. The film is about 30 minutes long, costs ten dollars, and is worth the time and expense. As a bonus, the theatre has a trendy bar attached, called the Black Dog Bar, that serves both drinks and snacks."

I said, "Ten dollars for a thirty minute movie seems a little steep."

Ron said, "Well, it's New Zealand dollars."

"That makes it cheaper for us?"

"Yes."

"But not for the locals?"

"I suppose."

After my insightful interruption, Ron continued, "Te Anau is the main jumping off place for the glacier-carved wilderness that is Fiordland National Park, and is located on the only road to Milford Sound, the main attraction in the park."

The scenic 2.5-hour drive to the sound was incredible. The weather was mostly overcast, but at times sunlight shined through to illuminate granite ramparts that ascended high into the cloudy sky—a massive backdrop of dark, foreboding gray to countless waterfalls that rushed down the sheer rock faces.

At the upper entrance to the Homer Tunnel, the bus driver pulled into a large parking area to wait for the all clear to enter the single-lane passageway. We left the bus to stretch our legs and gather photographic memories of the scenery.

After taking too many photos of waterfalls, I turned my attention to the muddy-green kea parrots that swarmed parked cars.

Ron said, "The keas like to loiter around areas occupied by humans, especially where trash is plentiful. The trouble comes from groups of young males—locals call them 'hoon' groups. Fueled with high energy food from the trash they hit the parking areas like marauding vandals, pecking out weather-stripping from around car windshields, and ripping off pieces of wiper blades to clean and sharpen their beaks or to satisfy a craving for its licorice taste. They are also known to tear apart motorcycle seats, and pick up cameras and cell phones left unattended, flying off with them, until they hover over a particularly hard, unforgiving rock, to drop the gadget, smashing it to smithereens."

Many drivers and passengers left their vehicles to photograph or just gaze at the scenery, unaware that the rubber-eating parrots were at work.

When it started raining, those who turned too late to watch the "cute" behavior of the birds, or to stop the demolition, were surprised to see rain dribbling down the inside of windshields, and wiper blades, sans rubber, etching the glass.

We finally entered the Homer Tunnel, and moved through darkness for almost a mile to emerge into the brightness of the Cleddau Valley.

Ron said, "Before the building of the road, Milford sound was a desperately remote community, accessible only from the Milford Track, which runs from the northern tip of Lake Te Anau. In the end, the building of the road was made possible by the cheap labor of men who could find no other work during the depression years of the 1930s. Their life in this remote, flood-besieged, and avalanche-ravaged land was immensely hard. Many died. The Milford Road is still threatened by frequent avalanches today."

After we arrived at the sound, which is really a fiord, we boarded the *Pride of Milford*, a large catamaran ideal for groups with large windows (not the groups) and viewing decks, for a two hour cruise.

I was looking forward to seeing a lot of snow and ice, since twenty years ago I had been prevented from reaching the sound because an avalanche had blocked the access road. But outside of a few waterfalls and a little snow high up, there was none of what I considered a classic fiord ecosystem.

All of the bare mountains and cascading waterfalls looked the same. However, the narrator on the boat tried to make things interesting by describing every rock, tree, and insect within sight.

He was big on sheep, mutton, and lamb, and even created some humor with a story about a ram that loved to travel to "become" a new "ewe" with each experience.

In addition, he provided more-than-I-wanted-to-hear information about farmers, dogs, wind farms, and small communities widespread along the way.

He interjected, "Movement here on left."

So many people rushed to that side of the boat, I thought we might tip over. Well, there was a definite tilt.

I spotted the subject of interest, a wapati deer that is prevalent on the South Island of New Zealand. This animal must have hung around with sheep too long, because he turned as soon as he spotted the boat, to "moon" us with his white butt.

Shortly after I settled down from that excitement, my interest was piqued once more when the narrator said, "Look at fur seals along the shore, chilling out on the rocks."

He added, "Only the male seals actually come into the fjord, the females stay out to sea. One dominant male gets all the females to himself, so the other males come down here, lie around, and beef up until they reckon they're virile enough to take on the head honcho and assume his place in the harem."

At least three times, he repeated directions, including where to eat, stand, and sit. He would have made a kindergarten teacher proud, but he overdid his zeal when he went into an explanation of the assortment of meals and refreshments on board.

For me, the captain created the most excitement. He had a habit of steering the boat from a small flying bridge outside of the main wheelhouse, so when I looked into where he was supposed to be, I thought we were in big trouble because no one was at the helm.

On the way back to Te Anau, we stopped at the Chasm. As soon as the bus was parked, the keas (not the cars) showed up, ready to do their work on any rubber parts. One even perched atop the open door. Fortunately, the bus driver stayed behind to thwart their repast.

Sharon and I, along with our bus-mates started up the trail. At the first footbridge, we stopped to view a series of waterfalls cascading into the Cleddau River.

We proceeded into a primeval forest filled with huge ferns, lush greenery, and hanging vines from lichen covered trees. At any moment, I looked for Tyrannosaurus rex to show up, but he would have to crash through the underbrush, since a force of several Japanese tourists, who pushed and jostled us out of their way, occupied the trail. Courtesy must not be big in their country, but thankfully, it hasn't infected the Kiwis (New Zealanders) who were always polite and helpful.

At the second footbridge, free of the Japanese who had moved on, we enjoyed a better view of the waterfalls crashing obliquely downward.

Thousands of years of swirling, crashing water through a deep gorge have sculpted shapes and basins into the brown, white, and green rock stratum, leaving some rocks hollowed and pitted where water had licked out the soft parts; looking like huge sea sponges.

I said, "Hon, look over there at the rocks that have been ravished so much they look like skeletons."

Sharon said, "I see what you are looking at, but you have a more vivid imagination than I have."

"Well, doesn't that stone over there look like a human pelvis?"

"A little."

Some rocks were covered with white material that looked like hardened, glutinous mucus draped over the surface, but I didn't mention that image to Sharon.

The next day, we traded our bus ride for a lengthy, pleasant but not spectacular, boat ride across Lake Te Anau to the Te Anau Caves.

We entered the caves at Cavern House, another name for the little visitor center, alias souvenir shop, at the start and end of the tour. That way, they get you coming and going.

Having little interest, I encouraged Sharon to leave the shop, rejoin our group, and descend underground to join a guided adventure by path and small punt through limestone caverns to the glowworm grotto.

While walking the path, ever downward, I could hear rushing water and knew it wouldn't be long before the path reached the shores of a subterranean river.

Sure enough, it happened. Having no path left to walk, I joined others in a small dinghy to continue the adventure. We drifted slowly along through an illuminated, beautiful underground world—a twisting network of limestone passages filled with sculpted rock, whirlpools and a roaring underground waterfall. The cave was cool, both in a shivering and superlative way.

Later, we floated in silent darkness beneath the delicate incandescence of thousands of tiny glowworms.

Breaking the stillness, the guide said, "A glowworm is the larvae stage in the lifecycle of a two-winged insect. It grows as long as a matchstick and looks a bit like a maggot. They glow to attract and trap insects brought into the cave via the river. The hungrier a glowworm is, the brighter it shines."

I asked, "How do they get their lunch?"

"Insects fly towards the light and get stuck in the sticky lines that the glowworm hangs down to catch food. These are drawn up and the hapless bug is devoured."

"It's so bright up there, I wonder if they ever get enough to eat."

"They do, and like the butterfly, they go through a cocoon stage to emerge as an adult that looks like a large mosquito. They have no mouth and their only function is to reproduce and disperse the species. Usually a male is waiting for the female to emerge from the pupa, mating takes place immediately, eggs are produced, and the cycle continues. Adult glowworms live no longer than a few days."

As I returned to the hotel, and in the days that followed, I couldn't shake the thought of the glowworms constrained purpose—to simply complete a life cycle over a few days—and of how nice it is to be a human being with a more innovative purpose, which I've yet to figure out.

Chapter 12

Quintessential Queenstown

Leaving early from Te Anau, we drove through beautiful sheepish countryside (sheep scattered amongst tussock clumps, as if they were trying to hide from us). There was no telling what they were doing behind the tufts.

However, Ron cleared that up, "The ewes may use the clumps to hide from predators, such as foxes, eagles, dogs, and even crows, especially when they are lambing or "tupping," or in the case of Dorper sheep, completely shedding their fleece."

"How decent of them," I said.

Ron said, "It's not a matter of decency; it's a matter of survival."

I was surprised to see so many domesticated Wapati, (white butt elk), that, like millions of sheep, turned their posteriors towards the bus. However, in some of the fields, sheep dogs were herding sheep so aggressively; they had no time to commit their obscene act.

As we travelled along, brilliant sunshine illuminated bright yellow gorse and light green quill-like leaves of New Zealand broom that stretched out to distant Manuka (honey) trees, and taller poplars and willows bordering the lowest reaches of snowcapped mountains.

At Kingston, a small town on the southern shores of crystal clear Lake Wakatipu, we paused just long enough to look over the vintage steam train called the *Kingston Flyer*—but not to ride it. Trains and rolling stock sat on rusted tracks, forlorn and out of use—unlikely to once again belch steam and smoke.

With thoughts of what it must have been like to journey on the *Flyer* at the turn of the twentieth century, I boarded the bus to ride with my mates to our first rest stop for coffee and "facilities" at the low end of Lake Wakatipu, where it is rumored that the "fishing is so good, you have to stand behind a tree to bait your hook."

Ron said, "Because of its unusual profile (shaped like a lightning bolt), Lake Wakatipu has a tide, or more correctly, an unusually large "standing wave," which causes the water to rise and fall about four inches every twenty-five minutes or so. Māori legend links this phenomenon to the heartbeat of a huge monster named Matau that is said to be slumbering at the bottom of the lake."

Just a few minutes down the road, we observed mist hanging above Lake Hayes, known as "Mirror Lake," because of its definitive reflection of trees and mountains in the waters on sunny days, but not at the moment we passed by. However, as we reached the pavilion, halfway along the lakeshore, everything changed—clouds lifted, and the sun came out giving credence to the lake's sobriquet.

We moved on to Arrowtown, New Zealand's only living historic gold mining settlement built on the banks of the Arrow River—once a rich source of gold.

Ron said, "In 1862, thousands of miners flocked to the Arrow River to the cry of gold. At the height of the gold rush, the population reached 7,000. While the miners have now gone, the legacy of those early settlers has been retained through careful preservation and it has become a treasure in its own right."

Lining a solitary street, single-story shops offer a sophisticated range of clothing stores, art studios, galleries, restaurants, and traditional pubs and bars.

Auxiliary to the street, lays the "required" Chinese miners village, or what's left of it—now stone ruins.

Standing on the semblance of a dirt road, I said to Sharon. "What is with these gold mining towns? All I have visited have at one time supported a Chinese community."

Sharon said, "That's true, but few of them actually panned for gold. Mostly, they "panned" the miners for their gold, by providing restaurant and laundry services."

"And opium dens." I said.

I wanted to try my hand at gold panning but we didn't have time, so I settled for searching for a shot glass. None labeled Arrowtown could be found.

Near Queenstown, we stopped for lunch at the Millbrook Country Club and Estates which covers two hundred hectares (approximately five hundred acres) of the Wakatipu Basin—a glacial valley bordered by the Crown Range, and The Remarkables, a mountain range that lives up to its name by rising sharply to create an impressive snow covered backdrop to the basin and Lake Wakatipu.

The resort includes three restaurants, a bar/cafe, a spa, and a 27-hole golf course—three separate nine-hole courses.

I asked a waiter, "Why the strange configuration of the golf course?"

He said, "I don't know, but I will find out."

When he returned, he said, "You can sign up for eighteen holes or nine, but not twenty-seven."

I said, "Then why have three nine-hole courses?"

"Well, you get your choice of which eighteen or nine you wish to play."

The situation didn't quite make sense to me. It reminded me of golf courses I played in California: Some eighteen-hole courses offered play on the front or back nine, other larger courses (thirty-six holes) offered a choice of either of two eighteen-hole configurations.

After lunch, we found our way to the Karawau River Bridge where fearless bungee jumpers dove head first from the overpass to just inches above the water, some one hundred forty-two feet below.

At times, it looked like the crazies could take a momentary sip from the water before springing upward, giving in to the recoil. Then, while they dangled upside down for several minutes, a small dingy was launched by two guys from the shore who rode out to unfasten them.

It was hard to watch. I feared the bungee would break and drop the dare-devil into the water.

Ron said, "If you want to be tied up and thrown off with a friend, then this is the bungee site for you, as it is Queenstown's only tandem bungee jump. Just remember that sharing the thrill doesn't mean halving the fear."

Sharon said, "Do you want to try it?"

"Tandem?" I said.

"No, silly, I meant by yourself."

"It looks like fun, but that heart-stopping leap of faith isn't for me. Besides, I don't want to tempt the fates at my age."

No one else in our group stepped up, so I felt exonerated.

We moved on to the Sky Ride, a gondola journey, reputed to be the steepest lift in the Southern Hemisphere, and more my speed.

Sharon was nervous about the climb and especially about the confines of the gondola. It was a tight fit for four people.

"It will be alright, Honey. Just look at me and not out at the scenery below."

"That works for me. I should be okay."

When the gondola car lurched upward, Sharon's resolve disappeared. She closed her eyes and forcefully clutched my arm with both hands.

The five minute ride to the top of Bob's Peak was exhilarating as the view expanded to a remarkable two hundred twenty degree panoramic vision of Lake

Wakatipu and Queenstown, accentuated by several towering peaks, including The Remarkables.

As we approached the top of the mountain, I wondered why such an unremarkable name was applied to the peak.

I asked Sharon, "Why just Bob's Peak?"

"How would I know?"

"Well, he must have had a last name."

"I'm sure."

"Maybe it was hard to pronounce or it was obscene."

"Only you can think up those things. I'm sure there were other reasons."

"Well, I think it would be interesting to find out."

At the summit, other daunting options were available including a bungy jump, a luge cart ride, and a paragliding flight.

Because the bungy leap looked more dangerous than the dive over water, I declined the offer to scare me out of my wits. This time, it was a plunge, one hundred fifty-four feet "into" the forest floor, that is, if you don't spring up at the last minute.

The luge (toboggan) ride, advertised as a chance "to get to know your inner child," offered a dash down the mountain—at your own risk—through natural and man-made obstacles, both marked and unmarked (how nice to let a rider know before hand). I did not try it.

Parasailing was another possibility, but once again, I deferred to heartier souls.

A walkabout on the outdoor terraces, some fifteen hundred feet above Queenstown, provided more spectacular views and great photo ops.

Crowds gathered at every turn, so I had to force my way to the edges of the balcony and find a way to avoid the "cobra heads" (smart phones) that always pop-up in my camera's viewfinder.

The only place that wasn't crowded was the exit. What a relief. Unlike the long queue we stood in at the bottom of the ride, no line formed as we walked to the boarding platform and entered a gondola for the trip down.

At the bottom terminal of the Skyline ride, Sharon and I "birthed" from the egg-like carriage. Looking left, I saw our group near a metal tunnel, the entrance to the Kiwi Birdlife Park.

Ron waived us over and the assemblage entered the sanctuary to slow down for a bit and take in the beauty of the natural world.

It was a short walk down a flight of steps into beautiful gardens including native trees, and ponds that enticed waterfowl. Under dappled shade, we strolled throughout the park to observe many of New Zealand's famous birds as well as the tuatara.

At home, an owl stared without blinking, a bird that looked like a pigeon on steroids clutched the branch of a dead tree, and a vulture drooped his head as if he had missed chow-call.

At the tuatara enclosure, a medium sized grey lizard that looked like an iguana lay lifeless in the dirt. Only one eye moved, watching a "horny" toad scurry about nearby.

All along the path, free-range birds of many sizes and colors aligned or ran about looking for lunch.

At the end of our meander, we entered, and found seats in an outdoor amphitheater to watch a conservation show featuring an owl, possum, hawk, pigeon, a stuffed kiwi, and the aforementioned lizard.

A trainer put each animal through its paces as she explained their attributes. While the owl and hawk showed their prowess by reacting to a swinging lure, the other animals just perched on a platform or on her arm; the kiwi was less than dynamic.

The tuatara garnered the most information from the trainer, "The tuatara are rare, medium-sized reptiles found only in New Zealand. They are the last survivors of an order of reptiles that thrived in the age of the dinosaurs some 200 million years ago. They measure up to thirty-one inches from head to tail-tip, and weigh up to three pounds. Their name derives from the Māori language, and means 'peaks on the back,' a reference to a spiny crest especially pronounced in males."

After the show, we visited the Kiwi house, where we adjusted our eyes to the darkness and caught the last feeding of the day. It was exhilarating to see the kiwis actually running about and into each other.

The attendant said, "This activity is a kind of flirting."

I said, "You'd think they wouldn't want anything to do with each other, especially the female, considering the size of the egg she produces."

"Well it's the irresistible call of nature, I suspect." Then, he continued with familiar information, but added something new, "The kiwi lays an egg that weighs one pound, equivalent to birthing a thirty-two pound human baby."

We stayed at the Queenstown Crown Plaza Hotel, which provided the usual amenities, including air conditioned guestrooms, digital television, wireless and wired internet access and kitchen conveniences such as a coffeemaker and well-stocked costly minibar, and of all things a pillow menu: *therapeutic pillows, soft yet supportive; European pillows, perfect for sitting up in bed; boomerang pillows, shaped to wrap around your shoulders, and feather pillows, made to move with you when you sleep.*

I chose the feather pillow because it sounded like the description of a perfect bed mate.

Although, all rooms were advertised as having an unobstructed view of Lake Wakatipu and The Remarkables, our room was on a floor that wasn't high enough to provide a clear picture of either, however, we enjoyed the view of the main street, the Sky City Wharf Casino, and some nondescript warehouses.

We left the room to check out the in-house services such as an inviting pool and an uninviting gym. Somehow, we ended up at the cozy lounge bar where the view was much improved. Refreshed, we left the bar and returned to our room

The next day we walked the downtown streets. Forget about souvenirs because Queenstown's shopping precinct caters to fashionistas at stores such as Louis Vuitton, and WORLD, which offers an array of luxurious fragrance and beauty brands as well as seasonal fashion collections including *on sale* trousers from $200 to $419 NZD, and dresses from $329 to $499 NZD. A placard at one counter says it all:

IF YOU ARE CHEAP
NOTHING HELPS

After a lot of window shopping at the large number of high street chain stores and local fashion boutiques inside pedestrian-friendly Queenstown Mall, Sharon purchased earrings and we retired to Póg Mahoney's pub for a pint and lunch.

The design and atmosphere of the pub was pure Irish. Lots of TV screens hung about for watching rugby, instruments typical of Ireland perched on a small stage, and a fireplace offered solace from the cold.

The ambiance plus the banter with the staff and other diners, especially those from Ireland, made us feel like we were in a different country altogether.

When a waiter approached, I asked, "How did they get the Irish motif so perfect?"

He said, "The pub was designed and built in Ireland and all the wood and bric-a-brac were shipped out from Dublin. As you'll notice, most of the staff are from the Emerald Isle, or at the very least have lived there."

The waiter handed us the refreshment menu and the dining menu, and asked, "Do you need time to look over both?"

"Yes," I said.

The first order of business for Sharon and me was to order drinks. The beer menu was extensive, including the famous: Guinness (not for the faint hearted) and Kilkenny (a smooth creamy ale), and the infamous: *Big Sky Brewing Moose Drool, Founders Dirty Bastard, Two Brothers Cane & Ebel,* and *Lagunitas Little Sumpin' Sumpin'.*

I thought about having a *Little Sumpin' Sumpin'*, but ordered an old favorite, Harp Lager, on tap. Sharon, who's not crazy for beer, ordered wine.

The lunch menu was also extensive, but not cheap. It included: *Homemade Beef Burger $23, Beef & Guinness Pie $24, Aoraki Salmon Fillet $31, Venison Fillet $33.*

I thought of ordering the salmon fillet, regardless of the price, until I read all that came with it: *served with lemon & dill cream cheese, roasted gourmet potatoes, crispy bok choy finished with a mint balsamic glaze.* So, like Sharon, I ordered the fish and chips.

Later, we went to the movies. I can't tell you what we saw—too many Harps, (the drinking kind).

Chapter 13

Cultured (more) Christchurch

When we flew in a private jet to Christchurch, I was invited to sit in the pilots' compartment where I observed the engine and flight controls, and the enormous dashboard full of gauges, knobs, and illuminated buttons, none of which I understood.

For a while, I talked to the pilots who never answered—their ears were covered with earphones. When I got tired of talking to myself, I finally stood up to leave, catching a glimpse of the outside through the cockpit windows. I was astounded; I had a more open view from my passenger seat.

I returned to my seat alongside Sharon, and faced friends, who, like some others rode the plane backwards.

After we landed, we toured Christchurch, the most English city outside of the UK. Shortly, we arrived at our abode for our two-day stay at the Crowne Plaza Hotel.

We enjoyed the amenities, which were the same as in the Queensland Crowne Plaza, and I was getting used to the different ways to flush the toilet—a push button that looked like the Chinese symbol for yin and yang. How appropriate that the struggle for existence between the two could be encompassed in a toilets' destiny; one side of the control for half a flush (philosophy), and the other for a full one. I couldn't tell the difference except in the push resistance—fast or halfast.

Cleaned up and ready to go, we left the room and rode an elevator downward. As is our habit, when we reached the hotel lobby we looked inward to see what was going on. Nothing caught our eye, except a pie warming seminar. Sharon showed little interest, and I couldn't see how warming pies could entice anyone to attend the event, so we moved on to the outside world.

An ancient tram, from out of the turn of the twentieth century, lumbered up. When it stopped, we grabbed the handrail, climbed the high steps, and stood next to the driver. He said, "You can ride all day and get off and on when you want."

We purchased a two-day pass, walked to the back of the carriage, and sat down on hard wooden seats, curved just enough to avoid a flat-ass syndrome.

I thought of my childhood experiences with the same type of streetcar that traversed Los Angeles in the 1950s:

> I lived near the end of the line for one route, and spent a lot of time—when I wasn't putting small rocks and pennies on the tracks to be crushed or flattened— helping conductors switch seat backs and clean up while looking (hoping) for loose change.

In Christchurch, the historic old trams follow a two mile loop around the heart of the city, stopping at sights of interest. We hopped off at the art center, a maze of studios, art galleries, theaters, cinemas, cafes, restaurants, and small shops selling everything from oil paintings to handmade crafts.

After we had pleasured our eyes with hundreds of artistic images portraying reality to abstraction, we lunched outside at the Dux de Lux ("Do de Loo" or "Duh de Luh"?) Restaurant, Bar and Brewery. The food wasn't much, mostly beer and garlic bread, in celebration of autumn, Sharon's favorite time of the year, but the people watching (one of our favorite pastimes) was superb. It looked like the teenagers and young adults were in the middle of the grunge-chic look: tattered clothing including thigh-hugging pants with cuffs shredding on the ground. Others wore knitted caps and garments like refugees from the Andes, or the Sherpa look from the Himalayas. Some adopted the Goth guise. One guy in his late 20s, sported a multicolored "Mohawk," arm in arm with a woman who looked like the bride of Frankenstein wearing boots with three inch soles that would make the monster proud. The best sight of all was a woman wearing a red turban, faux fur jacket, green "snuggy" leotards, and suede boots. Minus a much needed bra, her breasts drooped perilously over her large belly.

The next day, we punted (but not on fourth down) in a narrow, flat bottom boat on the Avon which is Gaelic for river, but often tourists and others add "River" to Avon, which creates the repetitious tag: "River River."

As the punt arrived, the punter, dressed in traditional Edwardian attire, helped Sharon into the boat, but I was on my own. I stepped into the vessel expecting it to rock, threatening a dip in the water, but the flat bottom kept it steady while I moved into position. It was a long way down, and I had some anxiety with my ability to rest my butt on the seat.

I asked Sharon, "Where is the damned thing?"

She said, "Keep coming."

As my knees moved closer to my chin I finally found a home for my own flat bottom.

"Higher seating is available," the punter said.

"Now you tell me."

"Would you like a higher seat?"

"Nope, I'm already down, and I'm not sure I can get up."

"Well, let me know. Also blankets, umbrellas, and hot water bottles are available so you can snuggle up with loved ones."

With cuddling intentions in mind, Sharon asked for a blanket, but we left the hot water bottle to others. After all we weren't that cold or old.

The punt, large enough to hold up to ten people, drifted smoothly along, propelled by a poling punter (sorry, I couldn't resist the alliteration), standing on a platform at the stern.

Fred Moritz, a good friend sitting near us said, "The punter is an American from Minnesota. He fell in love with New Zealand and a gal from the country. I don't know which came first. Anyway, he decided he did not want to spend the rest of his life on a farm in Minnesota, so here he is punting on the Avon while planning a wedding and searching for a 'real' job."

We sat back and enjoyed a relaxing thirty-minute exploration of the tranquil side of Christchurch. The watersides were at their best. Lush, tall grasses bordered much of the river, only giving way to willows, like overflowing fountains, cascading to the water's verge. Autumn colors were on full display. Maples and sycamores rose up in the background to parade gold, red, and yellow leaves, accompanied by a contrasting medley of trees bursting with green foliage. Birds fluttered from tree to tree, and colorful ducks made way as we drifted by.

As we rounded a bend, the foliage dropped away awarding a full view of Christchurch Botanic Gardens. The punter said, "The gardens were founded in 1863 when an English oak was planted to commemorate the marriage of Prince Albert and Princess Alexandra of Denmark. They give credence to Christchurch as the garden city at its very best because of the landscaped plantings, including at least 10,000 exotic and indigenous plants and trees."

After we paused for a while to gaze upon the gardens, we turned for "home." As we docked, my fears of getting up became a reality. I couldn't do it alone, so with the help of Sharon and the punter, I unhinged (physically not mentally) and rose to my feet.

Later, after a short tram ride, we found ourselves in Cathedral Square. Locally known simply as the Square, the area is the geographical center and heart of Christchurch, and has long been a community focal point, a place where people come together in good times and bad, and a backdrop for scores of significant historical events. Food is always close at hand whether your favored choice is ethnic fast food, sit-down vegetarian, or coffee and a bagel.

The daily market in the Square offers everything from Possum Fur garments, to affordable backpacker fashions, and greenstone—several types of hard, durable and highly valued stone found in southern New Zealand.

The wide-open plaza fronted and surrounded the turn of the nineteenth century Anglican Cathedral. As we entered the church, I noticed a small sign that advertised an offer—for a small donation—to climb the 133 steps of the Cathedral's North Tower, which dominated the skies of Christchurch.

"Honey, would you like to climb the tower?" I asked.

"Not on your life. You've got to be kidding."

Grinning a bit because I knew what the answer would be, I said, "Well, let's just look around on the ground floor."

"Okay, but it doesn't look as nice or as different from the hundreds of cathedrals we've seen."

Later, as we walked out of the church into the bright sunshine we made our way to one of the rectangular, raised tree beds that dotted the square, and found a seat on the shaded cement wall that bordered a large oak tree.

All manner of people were already sitting on the barriers under the spreading giant, seagulls paraded on the lawn behind us, and more souls gathered in anticipation of something.

A four wheeled fruit cart pulled by a van rolled into view. Finding his proper place, the driver stopped, got out of the van, and unhitched the wagon, propped the hitch on a wooden box, rolled back awnings on both sides attached to a peaked canvas roof, and revealed delicious looking fruit.

Obviously, this happening wasn't what the crowd was waiting for, since no one approached the portable stand.

In another direction, a long haired, bearded apparition wearing a flowing black robe and a "pointy," witch-like hat, approached.

I asked a guy sitting next to me, "Who or what is that?"

He said, "It's the Wizard of New Zealand, the most well-known of many colorful characters that entertain and educate in this public space."

As the Wizard unfolded a medium sized step ladder and climbed it to a position where he could hold the top step with both hands, he began pontificating about one thing or another to no one in particular.

My neighbor continued, "The Wizard is a New Zealand educator, comedian, magician, and politician. In 1974 he migrated to Christchurch and began to speak in Cathedral Square. The city council attempted to have him arrested but he became so popular that they made the square a public speaking area."

Since the Wizard spoke about things in a heavy New Zealand accent, it was hard for me to understand what he was saying, so after listening to what sounded like "wah, wah, wah," I gathered up Sharon and we returned to the hotel.

The next day, we rode the tram to Christchurch Botanic Gardens that sprawled over an area of fifty-two acres adjacent to the "River River" loop.

The Gardens display a variety of exotic and local plants of New Zealand, and collections of florae from all around the world including Asia, North America, Europe, South America and South Africa.

Our first stop, after we entered the Gardens, was, of course, at the visitor center, which houses a café, gift shop, and an interactive permanent exhibition featuring the history of plants and gardening in New Zealand.

Sharon was enamored with the section resplendent with every kind of gardening tools ever invented. She found a couple she didn't already have—a very narrow spade and even narrower one for digging weeds and grass out of cracks.

Happy with her purchase, she joined me outside. I had already left the place for "green thumbs"—of which I have none.

I thought about taking the narrated tour of the Gardens on board an electric-powered caterpillar bus, a one-hour, hop-on hop-off, open-top tour through the fifty-two-acre preserve.

However, Sharon was up for a walk, so we strolled through the urban oasis, and marveled at the colorful flowers, carefully tended lawns, massive trees, intriguing sculptures, splashing fountains, and water birds that caroused in streams and pools, where available.

With brochure in hand, we determined what was most exciting to visit of all of the different individual gardens.

Sharon wasn't interested in the Central Rose Garden that contained over 250 varieties of modern roses, nor the Heritage Rose Garden, a rambling collection of legacy roses, so we moved on.

One of Sharon's favorites was the Herb Garden (no relation to me), located by the Curator's House, exhibiting several plants of culinary and medicinal value. She rubbed and smelled many of the spicy plants, while I looked for cannabis—purely for therapeutic reasons.

We skipped the Cunningham House, a large Victorian glasshouse containing a sizeable tropical collection; Townsend House with its flowering plant displays; Garrick House accommodating an impressive cacti collection, but spent some time in the adjoining Gilpin House, walking amongst the orchid/carnivorous plant collection, where Sharon, a collector of orchids compared some and wanted others. My interest laid in the carnivorous plant collection, some big enough to swallow my hand, well, at least a finger or two. I didn't experiment. The plant reminded me of the one in the film, *The Little Shop of Horrors*, a farce about an inadequate florist's assistant who cultivates a plant that feeds on human flesh and blood. I must have stood in the fragrance too long because I thought I heard, "Feed me, feed me."

The highlight of this beautiful place is the begonia garden. Except for Monet's Garden near Paris, I have never seen so much beautiful color in one place—a vast array of vibrant colors, marked by placards that identified the varieties, such as Begonias' special; Gold Rush, Sunburst, and Angela Jane. (No relation to Mary Jane).

Sharon, a consummate lover of flowers, was ecstatic. "Oh! Look at the bright yellow one over there!"

As I followed the direction of her pointed finger, she said, "And the bright orange one over here!"

She kept up the patter, pointing to one vibrant flower after the next. By the time my eyes caught up to her directional, I was several flowers behind, so I gave up the chase.

We didn't have the stamina or the desire to visit The Fernery, (we have enough ferns at home), or the Rock Garden, (we're not into Zen), so we retired to a small restaurant on the grounds, and enjoyed a delightful lunch while we sat outside.

In the evening, we gathered for the last time as a group for a farewell dinner at the Canterbury Tales restaurant. It was fitting because of our own pilgrimage. The cuisine was international, New Zealand, and Japanese—take your pick—and the dress was smart casual. My clothing was casual but far from smart—too many times packed and unpacked.

I sat down and looked at the table setting: Dinnerware included three knives, three forks, and two spoons, a large plate, two smaller plates, and three glasses for wine, water, and whatever.

The introduction on the menu read:

Fresh ingredients, superb flavours, innovative presentation and attention to detail combine to create an exceptional dining experience and a journey that will delight your taste buds.

168

Upon looking deeper into the menu, it was clear that I would have to be careful of what I ordered in terms of courses (an eleven course meal was promoted) and description.

My concerns were realized with the explanation of the salad:

> Clevedon Coast Oyster organic apple air, seaweed salad beautifully presented with foam which here is called organic apple air. It's a juicy oyster with a delicate foam head.

And soup:

> This intensely flavoured cold consommé is strong in tomato with basil ice with a flavour burst from the balsamic pickled onion on a stick.

When the waiter asked, "Soup or salad?"
I said, "Neither."
Surprised, he left to take starting orders from my fellow travelers, and I returned to looking over the menu. The main dishes included:

> Pomegranate Seared Tuna, date terrine, salted orange, pancetta.
> Clearwater scallops, saffron cappellini, flying fish roe, candied citrus butter.
> Chai poached ostrich, chargrilled yogurt, melon slaw, raita dust.
> Tarakihi, jersey bennys, avocado, mango smoked prawns, rum raisin paste.

None of which appealed to me, so I kept reading.

When the waiter returned to take my main dish order, he said, "Our last savory plate is one that we are obviously proud of. It's artistically presented with the very tender cervena (venison) sliced thinly and seared lightly on the outside."

I said, "I would like the Barramundi."

He said, "The Barramundi is not available, and has been replaced by the New Zealand Tarakihi."

"What is that?"

"The Tarakihi or New Zealand Sea Bream, sometimes called the Jackass Morwong, is white, firm, and flavorful."

"Let me think about it, take other orders and come back to me"

When the waiter returned, I said, "I'll have the Jackass Morwong, naked."

He wasn't amused, "Naked?"

"Yes, without jersey bennys, avocado, mango smoked prawns, and rum raisin paste."

He was insulted, especially after what he considered appetizing descriptions.

He asked, "Would you like anything else with that?"

"Yes, French fries (another affront to the waiter and the elegant cuisine) if available, if not a baked potato with sour cream and chives."

He slumped like he had been stabbed in the heart, wrote my request down on the pad in his hand, and abruptly turned and strode off.

As the meal progressed, plates and silverware, used or not, were dutifully exchanged after every course. For me there was no exchange, the waiter simply removed the empty glassware, the silverware, except for a fish knife and one spoon, and the empty saucers. It was as if he was suggesting, "If you want naked, here it is."

Later, the waiter presented an extensive dessert menu that itemized treats such as:

Candied hazelnut and raspberry nougat glace on a sweet white wine and quince jelly, and black currant sorbet flavoured with ground fennel seeds.

I asked, "Do you have ice cream?"(Another mortal wound.)

He said, "Yesss."

"I'll have a scoop of chocolate."

He brought it, but he wasn't happy.

After dinner, Sharon and I spent time in the cocktail lounge listening to great piano music (another of Sharon's favorite pastimes).

In a last failed attempt to introduce the Cadillac Margarita to this part of the world, I asked the server if the bartender could make my favorite pick-me-up.

She said, "What's that?"

Rather than explain, I asked, "Can he make a special margarita?"

She responded, "What's that?

I gave up. I didn't want to confuse her any more by telling her about Grand Marnier.

"Never mind, I'll have a lager on tap."

Early in the morning of the twenty-first day, we embarked on the bus for the trip to the airport. On board,

Ron said, "I want to share a senility prayer with you that I got from a niece."

Then he handed out the single sheet of paper. On it was the following:

God,
    Grant me the senility to forget the people I never liked anyway.
    The good fortune to run into the ones I do, and the eyesight to tell the difference.

Below the prayer, he had added:

Have a great trip home. May the flights all be boring. May at least some of your friends wish to see your photos. May you remember what those photos are.
    Let's do it again somewhere else in this beautiful world.
    Love,
        Ron

The sentiments were right on, especially the phrase about some friends who might wish to see your photos (unlikely to happen), and remembering what those photos are. (I always keep a journal and along with a description of daily happenings, I label and number pictures shot.)

My eyes misted for just a moment as I finished reading the page. It was enough to make an aging traveler cry.

We left the company of Ron and our travel mates at Christchurch airport and flew to Auckland, and from there to Los Angeles.

At Auckland, preparation for the flight to LAX proved to be stressful. First we had to pay an exit tax of $25, and pass through a security checkpoint at the entrance to the gates. Then, while waiting for the boarding call, I visited a unisex bathroom. When I entered one of the stalls, a voice told me how to lock the door and how to open it. I was surprised it didn't tell me how to open my fly, urinate, close my fly, and put the seat down.

Finally, because we were flying to Los Angeles, we were subjected to a second security check before boarding. Once again, I had to remove my belt, watch, and shoes, empty my pockets, and present my passport. I wasn't a happy "camper."

On the Quanta's flight home on Saint Patrick's Day, I coincidently sat next to an Irishman named Lou Bagnus. He must have kissed the Blarney Stone because he entertained Sharon and me with some really good stories (all true of course).

At dinner time, I suffered through another "Yes, we have no bananas" routine:

The steward asked, "Do you want fish or lamb?"

I said, "Fish, please."

He said, "We don't have fish."

"Then, I will have nothing."

"Do you want a cheese tray?"

"Why not?"

I ate the cheese and crackers, and the salad that came with the tray, and an apple Bagnus gave me, so I was satisfied.

At LAX, we declared flower seeds we had purchased at the Botanic Gardens in Christchurch (of course the salesperson in New Zealand said the seeds were acceptable in the US). However, when we declared them the authorities labeled them contraband, treated us like we were stupid, and said we risked a fine or arrest.

I didn't know if they were serious or just having fun at our expense, so I said, "You want to punish us for being honest? It doesn't make sense; I could have just put then in my pocket and brought them home with no problem."

"Well, you should have known better."

The seeds were unceremoniously dumped into a trash can, and we moved on.

Coming home after a long trip is always a pleasure. Robert William Service said it best in his poem:

HOME AND LOVE

JUST HOME AND LOVE! THE WORDS ARE SMALL
FOUR LITTLE LETTERS UNTO EACH;
AND YET YOU WILL NOT FIND IN ALL
THE WIDE AND GRACIOUS RANGE OF SPEECH
TWO MORE SO TENDERLY COMPLETE:
WHEN ANGELS TALK IN HEAVEN ABOVE,
I'M SURE THEY HAVE NO WORDS MORE SWEET
THAN HOME AND LOVE.

About the Author

For over fifteen years, Herb Williams wrote a humor/satire column, titled "Life and Times," which was published in three California newspapers: the *Southeast Cities Tribune*, in Norwalk; the *Los Cerritos Community News* in Cerritos; and the *Redlands Daily Facts* in Redlands.

Some of the columns echoed thirty-two years of high school teaching and others reflected forty years of on the road experience including travels throughout all of the United States and Canada, several excursions into Mexico and Europe, and extensive tours of China, Australia and New Zealand. He has also been published in national magazines: *Trailer Life, Motorhome*, and *Trailblazer*.

His fifth book, *Echoes From Down Under* is a humorous account of travels throughout Australia and New Zealand.

Easy Writing Across the Curriculum or Anywhere Else, his first book, is a how-to manual containing a complete, sequential program of lessons and examples that can be used to facilitate the writing process in a non-threatening way.

North to Alaska with a No-Account Cat, his second book, humorously narrates a ninety day, 5,000 mile motorhome journey from Vancouver, British Columbia to Fort Macleod Alberta, by way of Alaska and the Yukon.

Only the Faces Change, his third book, satirizes thirty-two years of teaching in a public high school.

Where the Crown, Kilt & Shamrock Take You, his fourth book, romps humorously throughout England, Scotland, Ireland, and Wales.

Born in Maywood, California, Herb grew up in Bell and Huntington Park, served in the US Marine Corps, earned a Master's Degree in both English and Secondary Education at Los Angeles State University, and taught English, psychology and advanced composition at Montebello High School near Los Angeles, California. He is retired and lives in Redlands, California with his wife, Sharon.

www.ingramcontent.com/pod-product-compliance
Lightning Source LLC
Chambersburg PA
CBHW031301090426
42742CB00007B/551